Resurrection Knowledge

Resurrection Knowledge

RECOVERING
THE GOSPEL FOR
A POSTMODERN CHURCH

W. Stephen Gunter

ABINGDON PRESS
Nashville

RESURRECTION KNOWLEDGE:
RECOVERING THE GOSPEL FOR A POSTMODERN CHURCH

Copyright © 1999 by Abingdon Press

Library of Congress Cataloging-in-Publication Data

Gunter, W. Stephen, 1947–
    Resurrection knowledge : recovering the Gospel for a postmodern church / W. Stephen Gunter.
       p.   cm.
    Includes bibliographical references and index.
    ISBN 0-687-07157-7 (alk. paper)
       1. Jesus Christ—Resurrection.   2. Faith and reason—Christianity.
    3. Jesus Christ—Resurrection—History of doctrines.   I. Title.
    BT481.G85   1999
    232'.5—dc21   99-13583
                                                                                              CIP

The publisher gratefully acknowledges permission to use the following:

Quotations on pages 34-38 from *Church Dogmatics* by Karl Barth, ed. G. W. Bromiley and T. F. Torrance, published by T & T Clark.

Quotations on pages 39 and 40-43 from *Kerygma and Myth: A Theological Debate,* edited by Hans-Werner Bartsch, translated by R. H. Fuller, published by S.P.C.K. Permission granted by R. H. Fuller.

Quotations on pages 74-76 from *The Heretical Imperative* by Peter Berger, published by Doubleday.

The quotation on pages 80-81 from *The Way of Discovery* by Richard Gelwick. Permission granted by Richard Gelwick.

Quotations on pages 46-48 from *The New Quest of the Historical Jesus* by James M. Robinson, published by SCM Press.

Excerpts on pages 54-61 from RESURRECTION: MYTH OR REALITY? by John Shelby Spong. Copyright © 1994 by John Shelby Spong. Reprinted by permission of HarperCollins Publishers, Inc.

Scripture quotations marked NRSV are from the New Revised Standard Version Bible, copyright © 1989, by the Division of Christian Education of the National Council of the Churches of Christ in the United States of America.

All other Scripture quotations are translations by the author.

99 00 01 02 03 04 05 06 07 08—10 9 8 7 6 5 4 3 2 1

In Memoriam

Professor dr. Hendrikus Berkhof
(1914–95)

Church Professor Emeritus of Biblical and Systematic Theology
The University of Leiden, The Netherlands

HENDRIKUS BERKHOF taught through precept and practice that a theologian of the church can also be a theologian in the academy. Until disabled by a stroke after more than fifty years of active involvement in ecumenism, in the local and national church, and foremost in the theological academy, he seldom knew a month in which he did not ascend the steps as preaching minister. More than once when I visited him on Saturday, Corrie Berkhof would greet me at the door with an invitation that we share a cup of tea while "Henk finishes his sermon for tomorrow." While he did not preoccupy himself greatly in his writings with the seemingly intractable problems of historical reason and theological method, he taught all of his *doctorandi* that it was the conundrum that the nineteenth century bequeathed to the twentieth. Perhaps it is Berkhof's legacy to those who studied with him that we refuse to let the assumptions of the previous century go unchallenged into the one we are about to begin.

Contents

Introduction

Behind every book there is usually a story, and this book is not an exception. These pages are in part my intellectual story and in part a reflection of stories that I have heard from pastors and theological students during the last twenty years. Mostly it is a narrative about the intellectual journey of some of the more significant theological thinkers of the past two hundred years. To the extent that these people have been connected to communities of faith, this is a story about the church. This is where the "rub" occurs, and the friction of this rub might be posed as a question: To what extent does the formal theologizing in the intellectual academies inform the praxis of theology in local faith communities? Early in his career the famed Swiss theologian Karl Barth changed the title of his emerging systematic theology from *Christian Dogmatics* to **Church** *Dogmatics*. In a similar vein, this book is an exercise in what I have come to call ecclesial theology. It is of the church, by the church, and for the church. "Of the church" indicates that this is intentionally and perhaps even narrowly about the ongoing life of the believing body of people called Christian. "By the church" refers to the author being a person who does his writing with a full awareness that he is working out his salvation in the process of intellectual engagement. "For the church" points to the primary intended audience—not a particular denomination, but the *communio sanctorum*. This being said, this book also represents the academy for which scholarship is of supreme significance; and the intention of the book is to engage church and academy in conversation. As a theologian of the church, in this case a theologian in the Wesleyan tradition, being disinclined to this conversation is not an option.

Finding a common ground for conversation across academic,

confessional, and institutional lines is not an easy thing, but there is one common denominator that is present in all branches of Protestantism, as well as Orthodox and Roman Catholic expressions of Christianity. This denominator is Holy Communion, and across many faith traditions we share the liturgy known as The Great Thanksgiving, an important part of which is some form of the declaration, "Christ has died. Christ is risen. Christ will come again." These formulations are obviously Christocentric, and they affirm in one manner or another the saving work of God in Christ, specifically death and resurrection.

For the last two hundred years there has been an increasingly complex intellectual struggle over whether these affirmations are believable, especially in the sense that there can be any viable connection between what we know with our head and what we believe in our heart. It is here that anecdotal evidence is most evocative. Though such evidence is not conclusive in any social scientific way, the very existence of a large amount of anecdotal information suggests there is a significant problem that warrants address. Representative of this are conversations in recent years that the author has had with ministers across a wide geographic spectrum, one very recently shared in the sacristy of a large congregation prior to preaching and celebrating Holy Communion. A minister retired from forty years of service related in very sad tones how he was relieved no longer to be required to preside over a sacrament for which he could find no way to be intellectually honest. It required no coaxing on my part to get him to elaborate: "No one out there with any theological education really believes that the resurrection is true. I felt like a hypocrite for forty years acting like it is true. I struggled all my ministry to come to terms with what I learned in seminary...." I literally had to leave him talking as I began the processional to preach and lift the bread and cup saying, "Christ is risen. Christ will come again." I have had and heard of many similar conversations.

One was about a bishop, his son, and his grandson. It is a story about great loss. The grandson, at a rather early age, has died, and the family is stricken with grief. The church funeral service is past and the graveside service has drawn to a close. The grieving father goes to *his* father, the bishop who is relating the story, and draping his grieving self on the shoulders of his dad, he asks a question that strikes at the root of the historic Christian faith:

10

Dad, will I see him again? He is asking, "Is death the final word; is the grave the end?" As they console each other in their grief by touch and embrace, there is a long silence broken only by sobs before the bishop answers his son: *Son, I do not know if we will see him again. The church teaches us to* believe *that the grave is not the end, that death and the grave are swallowed up in the victory of resurrected life. But son, I just do not* know. *I want to tell you yes, but I just do not* know.

The teaching and preaching episcopal leader simply cannot bring himself to affirm the most central, fundamental historic Christian affirmation—the resurrection. Paul expressed it this way to the Corinthian church: "Now if Christ is proclaimed as raised from the dead, how can some of you say there is no resurrection of the dead? If there is no resurrection of the dead, then Christ has not been raised; and if Christ has not been raised, then our proclamation has been in vain and your faith has been in vain" (1 Cor. 15:12-14 NRSV). Affectively, the bishop clearly yearns to say "Yes!" to this apostolic kerygma, but there is a cognitive uncertainty that simply will not allow him to do so. This bishop is not alone in his dichotomized feelings—the affections inclined one way, the intellectual capacities trained to think otherwise. It is a question shared by generations of believers at the end of the twentieth century.

When I shared an early chapter of this manuscript with a bishop of my church, I asked him if this kind of intellectual dilemma were only a problem of the older generation, educated prior to the rise of postmodern thought. His response was, "The resurrection, so central in early Christian preaching and historic theology, has become a stumbling block for many pastors and laity who have been shaped by objectivism and rationalism. Here is an excerpt from a pastor [who] has surrendered his credentials because he feels he can no longer preach the doctrines with integrity:

> As for the uniqueness of Jesus as a historical figure, I have many more questions than I have answers, so that I can no longer preach with boldness, certainty or authority....I am tired of the feelings of intellectual dishonesty I experience every Sunday when I stand in the pulpit....We still have doctrinal requirements to guard, and I can no longer proclaim them, much less guard them.

The bishop added, "He is one of the brightest young pastors I know...who differs from many only in honesty. I find that many pastors have seemingly lost their faith. At least they lack a passion borne of conviction that what they preach and teach is true."

Intellection, Knowledge, and Belief

For most of its history, the Christian church has lived and worked out its theology with a frame of reference summed up in the Latin expression *credo ut intelligam*, "I believe in order that I might understand." *Credo*, from which we get our word *creed*, implies more than mental assent; it means also a sure abiding trust. For the Christian, this trust is in God. Implicit in this is the notion that native rational intelligence is limited in its domain, and that believing takes one in the direction of understanding *more* than if one does not believe. In this set of suppositions, knowledge that comes through faith is neither antithetical nor inimical to knowledge that comes more strictly through rational processes.

During at least the last two generations of believers, a decidedly different set of conclusions has held sway. At the risk of oversimplification we express this assumption this way: *Our intellectual, rational, empirical (scientific) ways of knowing provide us with true knowledge, characterized by greater and lesser degrees of certainty. Christian believers may assert that their faith gives them certainty, but this is of a religious order and may not properly be called knowledge.* One does not have to speak to very many college-educated adults or seminary students about this specific issue to realize that there is a broad intellectual chasm between faith and knowledge. *Credo ut intelligam* has been replaced by a separate compartment for believing and one for knowing. The bishop, the retired pastor, and the "resigned pastor" have plenty of company with regard to this chasm. Our faith, that is, what we learn at church, teaches us to *believe* one thing, but our intellectual heritage (in college, university and seminary) has inclined us to *think* otherwise. One might also say, the church teaches one view of reality and the "modern scientific" intellectual traditions have taught us another perspective on how things really are.

There is much talk these days that we are now "postmodern,"

as if the shadow and trajectory of modern paradigms change as quickly as the topics of our intellectual preoccupations. One of the characteristics of postmodern thought is that it gives us room to think differently than within the confines of the modernist split. My contention is that the great majority of us, even in scholarly guilds and academies, are not yet beyond the objectivist tendencies of the Enlightenment and Modernism's scientific preoccupations. The suppositions of Modernism are not dead, for three hundred years of thinking with a dominant methodology does not just disappear in one or two generations.

Re-Traditioning the Church

This book is about a clash of traditions, asserting that the church at the end of the twentieth century needs to be re-traditioned; it needs to learn and internalize again the historic Christian tradition, especially resurrection. For many the word *tradition* is inherently negative because it connotes that which is past, old, and outdated. It is decidedly not a compliment to be labeled "very traditional." When I speak of re-traditioning the church, I am cognizant of the minatory tones in which this call may be heard. I believe, however, that the potential gain is worth the risk. I have in mind the poetic word *remembrance*. I have in mind re-membering, for I hear and feel that we have been doing a significant amount of dis-membering. Just as an act of dis-membering a body can make it unrecognizable, so also the inability to re-member in new ways leads to loss of identity, to say nothing of distinctive identity. While it seems that the traditions of Modernism have increasingly *dis*-membered the historic gospel traditions, my goal is to pave the path for us to *re*-member and *re*-live the historic tradition: to move tradition from being the dead faith of the living to becoming the living faith of the dead.

In what follows there is an attempt to sketch a history of how we got where we are. After tracing a line of thought through nearly three hundred years, I propose how we can take a few more steps toward overcoming the intellectual "dilemma of our own making," steps toward being really postmodern. With regard to resurrection and tradition, this is not a "back to the Bible" speech in some biblicistic sense, but rather a plea that we find a way to recover the viability of historic gospel affirmation. If creatures and creation simply wind down to nothing or die and disintegrate, then, it seems to me, there is no hope for a future with God, unless we ground it solely in our existential imagination. For so many who go to church each Sunday, there is no longer any gospel of personal and cosmic redemption that is rooted in and arises from the whole presentation of Jesus as described in the Christian Testament. I wish to assert that there is a viable way to affirm these, but I have come afresh to this affirmation only after living intellectually *through* the objectivist historicism of the Enlightenment and Modernism. In a sense the morphology of Enlightenment historicism that follows is my story, and over twenty years behind lectern and pulpit have convinced me that many others have struggled *and still are* struggling with the manner in which historic Christianity has been historicized beyond recognizable remembrance.

There are several ways to move beyond the impasse created by objectivism and historicism, and one of these is to combine insights from sociology of knowledge with a group of assertions from knowledge theory—both of which were not formulated until the latter part of the twentieth century. The combination of these opens the door for a rational assertion that we know more than history by formal historicist definition will allow, and that rigidly defined objective knowledge has been surpassed in its value by tacit and personal knowledge. In the final analysis, we will be able to assert that the resurrection as taught in the Christian Scriptures and historically affirmed by the ecumenical councils of the Christian traditions is, indeed, true knowledge.

Chapter One

The Eclipse of Gospel Remembrance

The First One Hundred Years

When students ask me to define *postmodern,* I am often in a quandary. Usually I simply say that the reference is to *post-Enlightenment* in the sense that *modern* refers to our attempt to come to terms with the implications of the Enlightenment. But that is often no more helpful than labeling someone a liberal or a conservative, for it really depends on who is doing the asking. With regard to the Enlightenment and the church, I am not confident that modernism is really over for many of us, for the Enlightenment casts a very long shadow in the theological world. This is especially the case, I believe, when we look at the implications for the evangel-centered message of the New Testament as it is encapsulated by the Pauline assertion "If Christ is not risen, then our preaching is empty and your faith is also empty.... And if Christ is not risen, your faith is futile; you are still in your sins!...But now Christ is risen from the dead" (1 Cor. 15:14, 17, 20). Just how has the Enlightenment handled this central aspect of the NT kerygma?

The initial phase of the Enlightenment, or the Age of Reason, may be dated from the publication of Isaac Newton's *Mathematical Principles of Natural Philosophy* in 1687 to the Lisbon earthquake in 1755. The essential characteristic of this period was the widespread confidence in humanity's ability to understand and order the environment in order to achieve fulfillment: "The Enlightenment represents [humanity's][1] emergence from a self-inflicted state of minority. A minor is one who is incapable of making use of his understanding without guidance from

15

someone else. This minority is self-inflicted whenever its cause lies not in a lack of understanding, but in a lack of the determination and courage to make use of it without the guidance of another. *Sapere aude!* [Literally, "dare to understand."] Have the courage to make use of your own understanding, is therefore the watchword of the Enlightenment."[2] The interpretation of the Bible underwent slow but historically traceable changes when exegeted in the spirit of the Enlightenment, and this evolution has had a signal impact on what were once almost universally accepted tenets of the Christian faith.

The Enlightenment's first major impact on theology began in Germany. At the ripe age of seventeen, Gotthold Lessing departed the orthodox Lutheran parsonage of his parents in Berlin and went to Leipzig to study theology and prepare for the ministry. Preferring the theater to theology, he wandered, both intellectually and physically, until the year 1769, when he became the librarian at Wolfenbüttel for the Duke of Brunswick. In this setting he returned to his first calling and used the leisure of the situation to devote himself almost exclusively to the study of theology.

At Wolfenbüttel, Lessing obtained a four-thousand-page manuscript entitled *An Apology for the Rational Worshippers of God*, written by Hermann S. Reimarus, a professor of oriental languages at Hamburg, who had died in 1769. Reimarus never intended the pages to be published, for the questioning of orthodox tenets was rather unpopular. The pages were evidently penned as Reimarus' way of working through the issues for himself. Between 1774 and 1778 Lessing published seven excerpts from this work, giving as the title *Anonymous Wolfenbüttel Fragments*. In the "fifth fragment" Reimarus had rejected the resurrection of Jesus on the basis of the difference in the accounts of the Gospels. Lessing, obviously wishing to protect his own position, sought to distance himself from Reimarus' position by interpolating, "How much could be said in reply to all these objections and difficulties."[3] But Lessing then goes on to say that even if the objections of Reimarus could not be answered, the truth of Christianity lay not in the historical occurrence but in the soul of the believer.[4] From this point on, it becomes increasingly clear that Lessing's prime motivation for publishing the *Fragments* was to separate faith from the exigencies of historical proof.

The writings of the final three years of his life make this explicit. In his essay "On the Proof of the Spirit and of Power" (1778),[5] written in reply to J. D. Schumann, who asserted traditional orthodoxy on the basis of Jesus' miracles, Lessing rebutted, "Accidental truths of history can never become the proof of necessary truths of reason."[6] His foundation for this conclusion is a subtle distinction regarding epistemological categories that dates as far back as Plato's dualism. Plato used the metaphor of a dividing line to separate the two main segments of human reality: the world of thought and the arena of sense experience. Corresponding to the dualistic division of our world into the sensible and the intelligible realms is an epistemological dualism of the "contingent" and the "necessary." Contingent truth is known by sense experience, and necessary truths derive from reason. These distinctions are characteristic of medieval thought, especially that of Thomas Aquinas, and the Enlightenment generated a characteristically firm version of this dualistic epistemology, of which Lessing's is a reflection.[7] Lessing affirmed the historical fact that Jesus rose from the dead and therefore declared himself to be the Son of God, but he refused to base a belief in the deity of Christ upon the fact that he could not find any historical objection against the resurrection, for to argue from the resurrection to Jesus' deity was to argue from an accidental fact or contingent truth to a necessary truth (the accidental fact being the resurrection, and the necessary truth being the deity of Jesus). Lessing called this distinction between the accidental truths of history and the necessary truths of reason "the ugly broad ditch which I cannot get across, however often and however earnestly I have tried to make the leap."[8]

In the final analysis, the practical application of what Lessing meant is that all that happens in history is accidental or contingent, hence unrelated in any essential way to God, and it therefore cannot be the basis for believing an eternal truth, a truth so vital that its loss would be irreparable, like the deity of Jesus. Within this dualism resurrection is historical and contingent, which means ultimately nonessential. Christian faith is rooted only in what is essential.

The great philosopher Immanuel Kant followed Lessing in making a radical disjunction between faith and history. Kant constantly distinguished between the religion of practical reason, whose precepts are known to all through the categorical imperative heard from the depths of the soul, and historical religions that, while having many different forms, are essentially only approximations of this one religion of reason.[9] Essentially, Kant's categorical imperative is this: act in such a way that if the principle of your actions were to become universal, you would accept the consequences. According to Kant the categorical imperative provides every person with the knowledge of the perfect human being. Kant also affirmed that a historical record of the perfect human, Jesus Christ, is found in the New Testament. However, this perfection of Jesus, which lay in his inner disposition, could not be made manifest to others directly but only mediately through his teachings and actions. Since the knowledge of this inner disposition came by inference from his empirical words and actions, there would always be some room to doubt whether Jesus really was controlled by perfect motives in the inner reaches of his soul and was not just putting on a front of perfection. Nevertheless the categorical imperative, which we all have the capacity to possess, demands that we put the best construction on things so that we see in Jesus his ultimate perfection.[10]

Thus, like Lessing, Kant regarded the empirical stuff of history to be incapable, in and of itself, of conveying eternal truth, for such could be known only from the depths of one's own soul. He alluded to Lessing's figure of the wide ditch by asserting that between an objective fact (such as would exist in an historical report) and a concept in the mind there is no mediating analogy "but rather a mighty chasm the overleaping of which leads at once to anthropomorphism."[11] For Kant, Lessing's ugly ditch has become the Grand Canyon. To speak of the resurrection, in Kant's reasoning, actually discourages the living of the moral life, because "the elevation of such a holy person above all the frailties of human nature . . . hinders the adoption of the idea of such a person for our imitation."[12]

The Nineteenth Century

The influence of Kant can be traced in theological studies through various scholars of the nineteenth century, representative of whom is Heinrich Paulus, professor of theology at Heidelberg from 1811 to 1851. In the introduction to his *Life of Jesus*

(1828), Paulus revealed the influence of Kant when he said that he hoped his method of explaining away the miracles in the Gospels would not deter his readers from seeing that "the truly miraculous thing about Jesus is Himself, the purity and serene holiness of His character, which is, notwithstanding, genuinely human, and adapted to the imitation and emulation of mankind."[13]

Paulus argued that the miracles existed only in the minds of the evangelists, who, like the Jews of that time, attributed all phenomena to the immediate action of God. Nevertheless, the Gospel texts preserved certain details that provided the clue for their natural explanation. The resurrection of Jesus was really nothing more than a resuscitation. When Jesus was removed from the cross, he was not really dead but in a deathlike trance. When he awoke from his trance, he exchanged his grave clothes for those of the gardener, and so it was that Mary Magdalen mistook him. Summoning what strength he had, he wandered about for forty days, appearing to various disciples. During one of such meetings on the top of a hill, Jesus realized that he was about to die. He gave his disciples some dramatic words of departure and walked off into a cloud that had settled on the mountain. Although he had actually wandered off to die, the disciples believed that he had ascended in the cloud.

This imaginative stretch of rationality hardly made Jesus one to imitate, as had been taught by Lessing and Kant. It pictured him as an impostor who deliberately deluded his disciples. Rather than bridging Lessing's "ugly ditch," rationalists like Paulus had succeeded only in muddying the water. But the spirit of the Enlightenment to "take courage" did not die; it rather turned in a different direction—to Romanticism.

Beginning in the writings of Rousseau at the end of the eighteenth century, the mood of Romanticism became popular in the early part of the nineteenth, finding a theological representative in Friedrich Schleiermacher, especially in his treatise *The Christian Faith* (1830). For Schleiermacher religion was more than mere morality, a fulfilling of one's moral duty based on an internalized categorical imperative. The essence of religion was to love and to serve God, and the starting point (as well as the end point) for the knowledge necessary to doing this was the feeling of "absolute dependence." This feeling arises not only from the knowledge

19

that one is determined by environment, but also from the freedom that one has to shape and control environment.[14] But the freedom to do this determining exercise has been given to us in creation, and on this we must remain utterly dependent. It is from this feeling of absolute dependence that one receives the knowledge of God as the "Whence" of all things.[15]

Schleiermacher taught that Jesus Christ was the one who, though having the same environment and nature as other men, was unique in that he lived fully in accord with his absolute dependence. As a result, a community came into existence and still continues that, in mutual fellowship in looking to Jesus, finds in his example a redemptive power to live as absolutely dependent (para. 11). But the power that Jesus had and imparts to humanity through the church is quite natural, the natural power of a natural man or woman enabling them to own up to their absolute dependence on nature. The divine element in Jesus must be regarded "as an action of human nature, grounded in its original constitution and prepared for by all its past history."[16] The historicist approach to the resurrection is set aside, and the resurrection becomes a part of the ethos of the original and subsequent community that is rooted in the feeling of absolute dependence on God. It would seem then that the path of Romanticism following Schleiermacher held some promise for a foundation of knowledge on which faith could find a resting place. But this was not to be, for Romanticism's impulse did not take sufficient root to influence comprehensively the next generation of theological scholarship, at least with respect to resurrection and historical reason. When we move to the next two great figures of the nineteenth century, Hegel and Strauss, we encounter again the dead end of objectified truth.

Despite signal differences, we may look at the philosopher Georg W. F. Hegel in conjunction with Schleiermacher because he too saw the whole world as the expression of God. For Hegel God was conceived as spirit, as that which is pure identity and incapable of change. But spirit existing in and of itself implies a duality in which spirit is able to stand over against itself and look at itself. That aspect of spirit which transcends itself is universal in that it is able to view all of itself; but that aspect which is transcended can and does express itself in particulars. However, even a particular manifestation of spirit can transcend itself and see its universality. Spirit thus exists in a triad that is suggestive of the Christian trinity: "Father," spirit in its universal form, "Son," spirit in its particular form, and the "Holy Spirit," arising as the particular, transcending itself, and finally viewing itself as the universal. Hence the true meaning of God, or spirit, comes to light, for spirit is to be defined as "absolute reflection within itself in virtue of its absolute duality."[17]

To be sure, Hegel's way of thinking is abstract in the extreme, but there is a practical side of application for us. Individuals find a place within this concept of spirit, for we correspond to that second, particular manifestation of it; and we can be a unity with God when we learn to exist as true spirit, that is, when we learn to stand over against ourselves and to view ourselves as spirit—as being of infinite value and having an eternal destiny; in short, when we learn to view ourselves as having the freedom that is appropriate to God.

Hegel viewed the history of the world as the process by which the world, comprising the physical phenomena of nature and the psychical impulses of humanity, comes to express its freedom and oneness with God. With regard to humanity, it is here that Hegel's famous thesis-antithesis-synthesis formula comes into play, and it leads to Hegel's theistic interpretation of history. Humanity's understanding of itself as "free" has come about in three stages: in the oriental world the despot saw himself as free, but because no one besides the despot was free, this freedom manifested itself in capriciousness rather than in the good. The next higher level of freedom came in the Graeco-Roman world, where the aristocracy governed itself as a democracy. Here there was some freedom gained, but not all understood themselves to be free. The ultimate freedom was finally realized in the German monarchy of Hegel's time, and this was brought on by Christianity. The salvation of the world came in the person of Jesus Christ.[18] Jesus Christ was the first person to view his own spirit as capable of having unity with God. In order to demonstrate this for all of the world fully to comprehend, it was necessary for Jesus to die. By doing so it became evident that he had attained the freedom and infinity of spirit "by stripping himself of his finiteness and surrendering himself to pure self-consciousness."[19] Thus was launched the great idea of Jesus, that as man viewed himself as an infinite spirit he would realize his potential as a part of God. We too are called to

21

appropriate this ideal and accomplish Jesus' own history. Here are the very roots of the Idealism that shaped the rest of the nineteenth-century theological landscape.

It is clear that Hegel was a philosopher rather than an exegete or theologian, and he believed that accurate knowledge about God must be metaphysical. For this reason he interpreted the New Testament as pictorial language of the human imagination that was attempting to express ultimate reason. For Hegel, the resurrection theme of the New Testament was an imaginative way to express the permanence of what Jesus had taught. He explains the rise of the resurrection belief as a process. Gradually the disciples' grief over the death of Jesus subsided, and the spirit and image of his pure manhood rose, as it were, out of the grave. But along with this spirit there was the memory of his physical presence with them. "What was wanting in the divinity present in the loving community [of Christians] . . . was an image and a shape. But in the risen Jesus, lifted up heavenward, the image found life again, and love found the objectification of its oneness" in the concept of the actual resurrection.[20] None of this, of course, has any rootage in history per se, but it is a grand ideal which can be experientially lived out universally by those who emulate the life and obedience of Jesus. (We encounter a version of Hegel's "ideaism" in the twentieth-century concept of myth made popular by R. Bultmann.)

Thus it seems that Hegel, like Schleiermacher, was not troubled by Lessing's "ugly ditch," for God is to be found in the ongoing process of an idealized universal history. For a few scholars Hegel's Idealism held promise, and the ideal that we are capable of envisioning a grand narrative for all of creation and history has power still for a few. For most, however, its abstraction was simply too great and there was a return to the intractable problem of interpreting history. The most influential representative of this turn is David Strauss.

In his *Life of Jesus* (1835), Strauss made it clear that he was working from the historical premise of cause and effect. For every effect in the world there must be a natural cause. The resurrection hardly fits this assumption, and it is to the resurrection that Strauss paid the most attention, for he believed that "all the other miracles in the history of Jesus could be adduced as a consequence of the [disciples' faith in] resurrection."[21] After the death of Jesus, the disciples had a fixation on the Old Testament theme of Jesus as the Messiah, as evidenced by Luke 24:32, which says that their hearts burned within them when the Scriptures spoke of the Lord's life and suffering. Those experiences did, in fact, reflect the presence of the living Lord. The impression of burning increased in intensity until some of the more emotional followers actually had hallucinations of Jesus appearing to them. According to Strauss, the power of suggestion from these caused the rest of the disciples to hallucinate about the resurrection.[22] In Strauss' thought, Romanticism ultimately merges again with rationalism in the spirit of the Enlightenment, and with regard to the place of the resurrection in the kerygma, it founders on the assumptions of historicism. Only now we have moved far from the assumption of Lessing about Jesus' deity being the "necessary truth of history." By the middle of the nineteenth century, truth is to be found in the cosmic mind beyond history rather than in history. And the Jesus of the Gospels, who is clearly a part of history, is on the verge of disappearing as a source of historic truth for proclamation.

David Strauss had indeed taken the "enlightened" line of thought from Kant, Hegel, and Schleiermacher to its logical conclusion, but European Christianity found it impossible to assimilate this thinking even within the esoteric confines of the theological academy. Strauss had been appointed professor of theology at the University of Zurich, but the public outcry against his *Life of Jesus* was so great that the university, rather than letting him teach, gave him a lifelong pension. Strauss' rejection of factual history as a source for proclamation led several scholars to center their research on recovering the essential historical truths about Jesus that are available through the historical method.

Karl Lachmann set forth an argument for the priority of the Gospel of Mark in an attempt to show that the seeming discrepancies among the Gospels were not so great as many had thought.[23] C. G. Wilke, in his *Der Urevangelist,* and C. H. Weiss, in *Die evangelische Geschichte kritisch und philosophisch bearbeitet,* both took significant steps in strengthening the position of Lachmann. By using Markan priority and arguing that Matthean and Lukan narratives were theologized, the scholars hoped to define a historically reliable picture of Jesus. Subsequently H. J. Holtzmann advanced the argument that "Nowhere does the human Jesus emerge in such a recognizable fashion as in the

when one disregards the historicity of the Gospels — the Gospel becomes abstract — and overemotional.

Gospel of Mark."[24] His argument was that Jesus was the perfection of humanity: "No one will want to find another example like it in the history of the developing God-consciousness of man."[25] Since the personification of perfection was Jesus of Nazareth, he reasoned that Christianity was more than merely an "idea," for it was rooted and grounded, and therefore dependent, on its historical founder. Holtzmann felt that he could reasonably defend some of the "miracles" that Jesus performed; however, the "nature miracles" (the feeding of the five thousand, the stilling of the waves and walking on water) were not, by his own admission, accounted for. If only he could find a way to come to terms with the resurrection, then he would be able to come to terms with the vexing problem of historical analysis. In the final analysis, however, Holtzmann returns to the hallucination theory of the resurrection in his *Lehrbuch* (1911).[26]

Holtzmann provides for us a natural transition from the "lives of Jesus" approach to a theological approach, for he himself made such a transition when he went to Strasbourg to teach theology (1874–1904). The last quarter of the nineteenth and early part of the twentieth century was the "golden era" of liberal theology, set forth preeminently by Albrecht Ritschl, professor of theology at Göttingen from 1864 until his death in 1889. For Ritschl all theology centered in Jesus Christ, and like Holtzmann, he criticized Strauss for reducing Jesus to one among other great men. Jesus was absolute for Ritschl because Jesus had the God-given task of founding the kingdom of God on earth. In the life of Jesus, "that universal human morality preponderates of which the kingdom of God shall be the perfect realisation."[27] It was through the perfect obedience of Jesus that all humanity has been reconciled to God. Through Jesus the way has been paved for all to remain faithful to their vocation in the kingdom of God. We do not become totally like Jesus, for whereas we have only particular vocations in the kingdom, Jesus founded the "whole kingdom of God."[28] We accomplish our vocation through knowledge of our participation in the community of believers: "Authentic and complete knowledge of Jesus' religious significance—His significance... depends on one's reckoning oneself part of the community which he founded.... We can discover the full compass of his historical actuality solely from the faith of the Christian community."[29] In a manner similar to Holtzmann, Ritschl holds that the faith of the believer is the prerequisite to understanding the profound meaning of the historical Jesus. This premise is fundamental to the theological frame of reference for classically liberal theology at the end of the nineteenth century, and it was formative in the thinking of one of the greatest systematic theologians in the first half of our century, Karl Barth. The mentor who shaped the "early Barth" was Wilhelm Hermann, and it was he who, within the outlines of Ritschl's thought, devoted himself to making history foundational for faith.

Hermann was so convinced that Christian theology must free itself from subjectivism and align itself with the Jesus of history that he declared, "We Christians know only one fact in the whole world which can overcome every doubt of the reality of God, namely, the appearance of Jesus in history, the story which has been preserved in the New Testament."[30] The Gospels' presentation of Jesus as sinless was so overwhelming, in the thinking of Hermann, and they were of such foundation, that no conclusions of historical criticism could alter his certainty of the reality of God. One only has to look without prejudice to see "the clear portrait of a Personal Life that has no equal."[31] Not even the disproof of the miracles by the most sophisticated forms of historical analysis can shake the certainty of this reality. Should one argue that the historical factuality of the resurrection of Jesus is essential for the certainty and comfort that eternal life is the true end of those who believe, that would be a shaky foundation on which to build, for historical proofs provide only at best a greater or lesser degree of certainty. Besides, only a very few of the most intelligent and highly trained can even grasp such levels of ingenuity, and true faith must be equally the possibility for all.[32] Should one pose the question regarding how the believer comes to experience this certainty, once again the answer is found in the faith of the community that has grown out of the gospel tradition. The eyes of faith recognize the eternal verities.[33] Here again we see that the tentacles of historicism have Hermann so in their grip that he cannot extricate himself from positivistic historical assumptions, except to claim that the eyes of faith see what unbelieving eyes cannot see. Liberal theology is still alive and well, even though the problems of historicism have not been solved.

It fell to the son-in-law and former student of Ritschl, Johannes Weiss, and to Wilhelm Wrede to take away the remaining foundation stones beneath liberal theology's interpretation of Jesus. Weiss demonstrated that it was inadequate to interpret the kingdom of God primarily in ethical terms.[34] Furthermore, after the scholarly work of Wrede it was virtually impossible to accept the notion that the Gospel of Mark was free of the author's own theological bias, unless of course, one is willing to entertain the notion that Jesus was indeed theandric—both truly God and truly human.[35] Wrede made it clear that all three Gospels were permeated by "supernatural theologizing," and were therefore no longer usable as a foundation for liberal theology that, on the basis of historicism, had rejected the possibility that naturalism might be inadequate. If one were to continue to use the Christian Scriptures as a resource, and Jesus as a figure central to the Christian message, only one of two possibilities remained: (1) Either Jesus was truly the Son of God capable of performing acts that defy natural explanation, or (2) the supposition that he was such a person was so completely the conviction of the NT community that all of the accounts were theologized in such a manner as to be inextricable from the documents.

One had to choose between these two alternatives. Martin Kähler, professor of New Testament and systematic theology at Halle, chose the former, and Albert Schweitzer, then a young assistant pastor in Strasbourg, chose the latter. It was not Weiss and Wrede, however, who led Kähler to take the supernatural alternative. Weiss's book had scarcely appeared in 1892 when Kähler delivered before a pastors' conference a lecture whose published title, *Der sogennante historische Jesus und der geschichtliche biblische Christus,* stated the very alternatives that arose from the work of Weiss and Wrede.[36]

The two German words for "history"—*Historie* and *Geschichte*—helpfully describe two different ways of knowing or defining history. *Historie* is history that is known through the application of the historical method, which revolves around three principles: (1) the principle of criticism, which means that our judgments about the past cannot simply be classified as true or false but must be seen as claiming only a greater or lesser degree of probability and as always open to revision; (2) the principle of analogy, which means that we are able to make such judgments of probability only if we presuppose that our own present experience is not radically dissimilar to the experience of past persons;

and (3) the principle of correlation, which means that the phenomena of history are so related and interdependent that no radical change can take place at any one point in the historical nexus without effecting a change in all that immediately surrounds it.[37] In contrast to this more deductive way of knowing history, *Geschichte* is known when one recognizes the reality or truthfulness that inheres in the story told, or, as some theologians have asserted, when one is apprehended by the reality that is foundational to the accounts.

Kähler insisted that to find the real Jesus it is necessary to begin where the New Testament writers began, with the Jesus who had actually risen and ascended to heaven. Refusing steadfastly to begin with the moralism of liberal theology, Kähler asserted that Jesus was the glorified Lord "not because his earthly life had made such an impression upon their soul, but because the resurrection first placed this earthly life in its proper perspective and gave it implicit and appropriate content."[38] Whereas in liberal theology the true Jesus was somewhere behind what we might call the "theological coloring book" of the writers, Kähler insisted that "the resurrected Lord is not the historical *(historisch-)* Jesus behind the Gospel, but the Christ of apostolic preaching, which is the content of the whole New Testament" (p. 41). Furthermore, both the Gospels and the epistles set forth the risen Lord (pp. 63-64), although the Gospels have the unique function of showing that the risen Lord was the Word who had become flesh (pp. 34-35). Thus the truly historic *(geschichtlich)* Jesus is the resurrected Lord, and Kähler concluded that the Gospels do not give us a distorted picture of him as he was during his earthly ministry when they set forth his miracles, his apocalypticism, and his Messianic consciousness. For during that ministry he was the Word made flesh who would rise from the dead and ascend into heaven.

Albert Schweitzer, in *The Secret of the Messiahship*,[39] sought to explain the Messiahship of Jesus, not in terms of the Messianic secret as a creation of the early church, but as a personal conviction of Jesus himself that began at the moment of his baptism, the moment when he realized his solidarity with God (pp. 6-7). As to why Jesus kept this a secret from those closest to him, Schweitzer proposed that the public announcement was contingent upon the eschatological appearance of the kingdom: "Jesus' Messiahship . . . was a secret, inasmuch as it could be realised only

27

at a definite time in the future....It was enough if by his word and his signs he might convert them to faith in the nearness of the kingdom, for with the coming of the kingdom his Messiahship would be manifest" (p. 186).

In 1906 Schweitzer published the tome *Von Reimarus zu Wrede*.[40] Although he made some strides with regard to the issue of the secret Messiahship, emphasizing the concept of Jesus' self-understanding posed the distressing question of whether Jesus had true insight or whether he was deluded. Schweitzer chose the latter: "Jesus...in the knowledge that He is the coming Son of Man, lays hold of the wheel of the world to set it moving on that last revolution which is to bring all ordinary history to a close. It refuses to turn, and He throws Himself upon it. Then it does turn; and crushes Him. Instead of bringing in the eschatological conditions, He has destroyed them. The wheel rolls onward, and the mangled body of the one immeasurably great man, who was strong enough to think of Himself as the spiritual ruler of mankind and to bend history to His purpose, is hanging upon it still" (pp. 368-69). A corpse is all that we have left.

And Schweitzer goes yet further by saying that the life of Jesus was not "a help but perhaps even an offense to religion" (p. 399). And still further by asserting, "The abiding and eternal in Jesus is absolutely independent of historical knowledge and can only be understood by contact with His spirit which is still at work in the world" (p. 399). This is a far cry even from the position of Strauss that earned him a life-long pension from the University of Zurich, for, as far as I am aware, no other previous scholar in the history of Jesus research went so far as to make the Jesus of history an offense to religious belief.

A review of our story to this point underscores some truly significant shifts in theological thinking from the latter part of the eighteenth to the end of the nineteenth century. The challenge of the Enlightenment to take personal courage and seize the moment to move beyond the status quo for human freedom and individuality set off a chain of reactions that were beyond anticipation. When Lessing posited Christianity's veracity in the soul of the individual, he clearly had no inkling of rampant subjectivity and relativism. Indeed, his intention was to provide a safe haven for the historic faith against the threats of historical reason. Lodging the place of safety with the individual seemed to be the only safe move, and Immanuel Kant buttressed this by suggesting that the categorical imperative of moral behavior as supremely represented in Jesus was the supreme imitable pattern for every human being. The implication that individuals are naturally capable of imitating Jesus, however, was catastrophic with regard to the NT narratives about the death/resurrection of Jesus—for imitating the resurrection is clearly absurd. With regard to moral behavior the categorical imperative is comprehensively relevant, but the gospel of Jesus Christ may not be reduced to moralism.

Be this as it may, Kant's influence over the nineteenth century is pervasive; hence, Heinrich Paulus believed the absence of anything miraculous about the life of Jesus did not change the "truly miraculous" about Jesus: "the pure, serene holiness of his character." All references to Jesus being fundamentally other than human are explained away—ascension becomes wandering off lost in a low-hanging cloud to die, for resurrection was really resuscitation and the disciples fabricated the rest.

The romanticism of Schleiermacher and the idealism of Hegel essentially changed nothing with regard to the academy's ongoing dis-membering of the gospel, and the nineteenth century ended in a conservative-liberal split. The closest thing to a rapprochement was Martin Kähler's distinction between the "so-called historical Jesus" and the "historic biblical Christ." The result was, however, that the foremost centers of theological inquiry in Europe and the U.S. at the end of the nineteenth century could only be described by the word *liberal*. The assumption was that resurrection does not conform to the canons of historical reason and therefore must be untrue.

Chapter Two

Giants in the Land

In the previous chapter we outlined the legacy that nineteenth-century (largely) German research bequeathed to modern scholarship, and it is with this background in mind that one must read the early theology of (arguably) the greatest theologian in the first half of this century, Karl Barth. This was an age when German *Kultur* was deemed to be superior to all others, and, in fact, following Hegel, believed to be a synthesis point in world history. It was a culture to be cultivated and spread, even if by war and armed conquest. Thus when Adolf Harnack, one of Barth's teachers, spoke to a gathering in Berlin on August 11, 1914, a week after Belgium had been invaded, he said: "Our *Kultur* is the most precious possession of humanity...and we pledge our wealth and our blood to the last drop for this *Kultur*."[1] It was this same cultural aristocentricity that led ninety-three German intellectuals to sign a petition on October 3, 1914, entitled *An die Kulturwelt* ["To the World Culture"], which supported the war policies of Kaiser Wilhelm II that had so recently included the killing of passive Belgian civilians and the destruction of the library at Louvain: "We will fight this war to the end as a people of *Kultur*, to whom the legacy of a Goethe, a Beethoven, and a Kant is just as holy as its hearth and soil."[2]

Karl Barth (a native Swiss, educated and teaching in Germany) read these words in the paper the next morning. He thereafter referred to October 4 as a "dark day" in history. As he relates, the names of his honored teachers, including Hermann and Harnack, were affixed to the document: "I found to my horror the names of nearly all my theological teachers whom up to then I had religiously honored. Disillusioned by their conduct, I perceived that

31

I would not be able to accept their ethics and dogmatics, their biblical exegesis, their interpretation of history, that at least for me the theology of the 19th century had no future."[3] It was Barth's total disillusionment with all of his German educational and cultural past that spurred him to strike out in a new direction. He turned to the Danish philosopher Søren Kierkegaard, whose work had been eclipsed in popularity by Hegel. In the second edition of his *Römerbrief*, Barth said: "If I have a system, it is limited to a recognition of what Kierkegaard called 'the infinite qualitative distinction' between time and eternity, and to my regarding this as possessing negative as well as positive significance: 'God is in heaven, and thou art on earth.' "[4] Barth's disillusionment with his mentors was only reinforced by the carnage of World War I, and he became totally convinced of the "inhumanity of humanity." Barth commented that whatever humanity or morality might be at our disposal comes from "beyond all human possibilities, whatsoever they may be" (p. 159). Barth concluded, against liberal theology, that the life of Jesus was not an exaltation of humanity but rather a manifestation that through the death of Jesus, God was saying a complete and final "NO!" to all the possibilities of this world.

However, this "No" of death is accompanied by the "YES!" of the resurrection, which opens up the knowledge of the kingdom of God. The dilemma of such an assertion, for Barth and still for us, is *how one gains knowledge of the resurrection*. This question is at the heart of Barth's exegesis of Romans, and in carrying out this task he insists that we are not to rely upon the "preliminary" results of history, but rather turn to the "creative energy" which enables us "with intuitive certainty" (p. 7) to break down the walls that separate the first from the twentieth century, so that we are confronted with the heart *(die Sache)* of the issue, the wholly other God who confronts us in Jesus Christ (p. 10). Historical research may throw light on the social context and etymology of Paul's words, but historical analysis does not introduce one to Jesus Christ. Barth thinks back to his days as a pastor in Safenwil, and he knows that whatever hermeneutic he applies, it must liberate and enable one to preach the gospel: "I myself know what it means year in year out to mount the steps of the pulpit, conscious of the responsibility to understand and to interpret, and longing to fulfil it; and yet, utterly incapable, because at the

University I had never been brought beyond that well-known 'awe in the presence of History' which means in the end no more than that all hope of engaging in the dignity of understanding and interpretation has been surrendered" (p. 9).

The affinity between Barth and Kähler is readily apparent, but they are not saying the same thing. You will remember that for Kähler the reason for believing the resurrection of Jesus was his matchlessness that shines through the entire New Testament, a reality graspable by human reason. But Barth insisted that faith was totally and completely the work of God with *absolutely no foundation* in human reason. It comes "from the other side" and is not continuous with anything in humanity or the world.

In the initial stages of this movement, known as dialectical theology, Barth was joined by several others who later made a significant impact on the twentieth century: Friedrich Gogarten, Emil Brunner, and Rudolf Bultmann. This quartet of theologians did not remain together, however, and it is the personal and literary debate between Bultmann and Barth that is of specific interest for our topic, for both were concerned with the historicity of the resurrection and both remained until their deaths vitally interested in the task of preaching. We will see shortly that they went totally separate directions after World War II, but the seeds of the separation were already present in the 1920s. In 1924 Barth wrote *Die Auferstehung der Toten*,[5] a treatise on First Corinthians using the resurrection of the dead as an interpretive theme. Barth's understanding of the resurrection had undergone little change since his commentary on Romans. In this later piece he argues that Paul's purpose in speaking of resurrection in 1 Corinthians 15:1-9 was not to give any historical verification for this event but rather to show that the message he had preached to the Corinthians was the same as that of the primitive church—Jesus Christ, the risen Lord and Savior of humanity (p. 138).

Bultmann reacted by accusing Barth of "false exegesis," for Bultmann was moving in the direction that would later give basis for his more existential handling of the text: "I can only understand 1 Cor. 15:1-9 as [Paul's] attempt to make credible [to the believers] the resurrection of Christ as an objective historical event."[6] Here we see Bultmann's concern for the "believability" of the event from a human perspective, a perspective for which Barth, as later becomes perfectly clear, has only the greatest of disdain. Both agree that Paul is getting at the heart of the kerygma here, but it was Bultmann's growing insistence that the knowledge of the resurrection must be thoroughly existential, a moment-by-moment experience (p. 64), that drove the final wedge between them.

Barth made a "false start" at writing a systematic theology in 1927, *Die Lehre vom Worte Gottes: Prolegomena zur christlichen Dogmatik [The Doctrine of the Word of God: An Introduction to Christian Dogmatics]*, in which, as he later confesses in the foreword to his *Die kirchliche Dogmatic* (1931–65) [*Church Dogmatics* (1956–69)], he was much too dependent on the existentialism of Kierkegaard and thereby left the door open for the human-centeredness of Schleiermacher, Ritschl, and Hermann. Notice the change from "Christian" to "church" dogmatics. For Barth the word *Christian* connoted the human and experiential aspect of Christianity, whereas *church* places us under the Word of God. With this move he has broken once and for all with any notion of theology being done "from below," i.e., from the human side. From this time on Barth's theology is often described by historians of doctrine as "the later Barth," and if one reads the *Dogmatics* with these differences in mind, it is readily apparent that the differences are significant, not the least of which is his increased discussion of the resurrection.[7]

Barth came to the conclusion, like Troeltsch before him, that such a view of history leads inevitably to a theological agnosticism which refuses to take seriously the unique revelation of the knowledge of God in Jesus Christ. It is an interesting theological exercise to see how Barth attempted to unfold the "objective knowledge of God that he believes is given to man in a real historical event."[8] This transition from a nonobjective to an objective view of history brings Barth into increasing conflict and polemic with Bultmann.[9] Although he commends Bultmann for the central position he gives the resurrection in the New Testament, he also criticizes him for doing away with its objectivity and reality. Barth maintains that this deletion is crucial. The proclamation "in Jesus' name" derives from the *fact* that Jesus entrusted it to the disciples *after* he was raised from the dead.[10] Not only did the disciples have an "objective encounter" with Jesus (p. 444), this Jesus was bodily, physically, raised from the dead (p. 448). Bultmann's practice of calling the resurrection a "nature miracle" is, Barth feels, "splitting hairs" (p. 451). Instead of helping to explain the event, this only makes it more difficult. The event could not have been what it was—God Himself, the Creator, manifested in the resurrection—unless it "genuinely and apprehensibly" included nature and, therefore, was physical (p. 451). But the event was not only physical, for Jesus also appeared to them "in the mode of God" (p. 448). The witness of the early church is unequivocal in asserting the bodily character of the resurrection. This is the whole point of the tradition of the forty days when he "came and went among them," when they "saw and touched and heard," when he "ate and drank with them." Furthermore, "unless Christ's resurrection was a resurrection of the body, we have no guarantee that it was the decisively acting Subject Jesus Himself, the *man* Jesus, who rose from the dead" (p. 448). Hence, the New Testament accounts of the empty tomb and of the physical appearances are indispensable; they cannot be omitted or explained away:

> It may and must be said, not as a postulate but as a legitimate explanation of the facts, that if the man Jesus was the incarnate Word of this God, if as such he was the Bearer of a hidden glory, . . . and if finally this hidden declaration of His nature was to be effective as well as operative, if it was not to remain hidden but to be disclosed, then everything had to happen as it actually did according to the Easter story in its simple, literal sense. There was no other way. (p. 451)

Immediately the questions are posed: Are we not right back were we started? Is Barth not saying exactly what orthodoxy has maintained for centuries? In the light of the development of the historical-critical method, is Barth not asking for a sacrifice of the historian's intellect? To each question, Barth's answer is a definite "No!" The Easter story has always been "incredible," not only to the sophisticated Areopagites but also to the unsophisticated disciples. There is no reason why it should be more credible in the twentieth century than then; but, at the same time, "there is no real reason why it should not be accepted freely and gladly even to-day" (p. 447). Indeed, the worldview and mentality of modern man, which are so incompatible with the inclination to "gladly accept," should not be allowed to prejudge "in advance and unconditionally our acceptance or rejection of the biblical message" (p. 447).

When we remember the position which the "early Barth" once held, we are forced to ask how he himself answers his "earlier" questions with his own "later" answers. It is just at this point that he becomes vague. The question which Bultmann tries to answer in an entirely different way is still haunting Barth: "Is it true that an event alleged to have happened in time can be accepted as historical only if it can be proved to be a ' "historical" fact' in Bultmann's sense?—i.e., when it is open to verification by the methods, and above all the tacit assumption, of modern historical scholarship?" (p. 446). On this basis Bultmann can reject the forty days tradition (and others also) because they do not fit the description given to "historical facts," in the strict sense of the term. Now Barth proposes his own answer, and he begins by agreeing with Bultmann:

> He is right enough in this, for it is quite impossible. But he jumps to a false conclusion when he insists that for this reason the facts reported could not have occurred. History of this kind may well have happened. We may well accept as history that which good taste prevents us from calling " 'historical' fact," and which the modern historian will call "saga" or "legend" on the ground that it is beyond the reach of his methods, to say nothing of his unavowed assumptions. It belongs to the nature of the biblical material that although it forms a consecutive historical narrative it is full of [a qualitatively different] kind of history and contains comparatively little "history" in Bultmann's sense. (p. 446)

From his own testimony we know what he means by Bultmann's sense of history, but it is not yet clear what Barth means by "history." He has spoken above of the "objective encounter" the disciples had with Jesus when he had been physically resurrected from the dead. Now he seems to be saying that these "objective events" cannot be "objectively verified." They occurred in time and space, but they cannot be verified in time and space. But they can be verified! He continues, "We must still accept the resurrection of Jesus, and His subsequent appearances to His disciples, as genuine history in its own particular time" (p. 447). This particular time is a subsequent time, the time which Jesus was given after his normal time was spent. In "His time" he reappeared! The only appropriate language to describe such a reality is the language of poetry and saga: "For they are describing an event beyond the reach of historical research or depiction" (p. 452).

The title of this section of the *Church Dogmatics* provides, as always, the key to what Barth is trying to say: "Jesus, Lord of Time." The only true reality, historical or otherwise, which confronts man is Jesus. He is the Subject, and he is beyond verification in our time. He is also the Object, and he will not be walled in by historical canons. He is the locus of history, the primary locus, the single locus. This, then, is Barth's answer to the question of how revelation occurs in history. He has proposed a special objective history, beyond the normal objective history, which cannot be verified by objective means. One is left with the feeling, as Van Harvey has expressed it, that Barth "leaves the inquirer in the position of having to accept the claims of alleged eyewitnesses or risk the state of being a faithless man."[11] Harvey, like many other students of Barth, is misreading him at this point. Even when Barth seems to be saying this, it is not what he means when he describes "the very nature of the events" under consideration that are "God's activity." Barth is asserting something quite different, namely, that this saving work of God cannot be reduced in its dimensions to the qualification and limitations of human rationality.

What Barth is offering us is "reasonableness beyond reason." In a particularly illuminating section in *Church Dogmatics* I/1, he asserts that it is impossible for us to identify (make equal) the Word of God with either the "secular form" in which the divine content veils itself or the "divine content" in absence of secular form—for the Word of God contains simultaneously both form and content. The "event of the Word" is an occurrence in which there is a synthesis of form and content, but this duality of form and content cannot be manufactured by any human being. It is in this assertion that we perhaps see the dialectical nature of Barth's theology most starkly expressed:

> It is a matter of hearing the whole, the real Word of God, and therefore, both the *unveiling* of God in His veiling as well as the *veiling* of God in his unveiling. The secular form with the divine content is not the Word of God and the divine content without the secular form is also not the Word of God. We can neither stop at the secular form as such nor can we fly off beyond this and try to enjoy the divine content alone. The one would be realistic

theology, the other idealistic theology, and both bad theology....
The coincidence of the two is clear to God but not discernible by
us. What is discernible by us is always form without content or
content without form. Our thinking can be realistic or idealistic
but it cannot be Christian. Obviously the concept of synthesis
[worked out by us] would be the least Christian of all, for it would
mean no more and no less than trying to achieve God's miraculous
act ourselves.... Faith means recognizing that synthesis cannot be
attained [by us] and [this leads to our] committing it to God and
seeking and finding it in Him.[12]

Commenting on this passage and the dialectical nature of
Barth's theological enterprise, McCormack sums up the Barthian
premise: "In and of ourselves, our thinking in the face of the
Word can only be realistic or idealistic thinking.... If we seek to
go beyond these human possibilities—if we seek to achieve a synthesis of the two—we are seeking that which is beyond the realm
of human possibility. Where genuine synthesis of the secular form
and the divine content has occurred, there human efforts have
ceased. There the miracle has occurred; God has acted."[13] With
regard to this, there are two crucial points for our discussion that
need to be highlighted. First, Barth's dialectical theological enterprise, for all of his own protest against liberalism and modernism,
is a thoroughly *modern* undertaking. He has not escaped rationalism fully; he is still firmly held, albeit on the banks of the
Rhine and not the Jabbok, in a Jacobean struggle to free himself
from the historicist assumptions that dictated the perspective of
Ernst Troeltsch. He simply tries to transcend Troeltsch by posit-
ing a qualitatively different kind of history, Jesus in "His time."
Second, equally modern and comprehensively influential, the
legitimacy of Kantian epistemology is pervasively accepted. It is
from the duality of Kant's perspective that we get Barth's language of "veiling and unveiling" in God's Self-revelation.

Barth's history beyond historical reason led to intense and
direct conflict with many of his contemporaries, most of all the
other "giant" on the theological scene in the mid-twentieth century, Rudolf Bultmann. Bultmann's famous essay "The New
Testament and Mythology," which spells out his concept of
myth, is pivotal for his system of thought as a whole, but to truly
understand what Bultmann has tried to do with the problem of
history and the attendant gospel issue of resurrection, we must

also turn to the 1955 Gifford Lectures, which have been published in Great Britain under the title *History and Eschatology* and in the U.S. as *The Presence of Eternity*. He lays down a principle in those lectures which must constantly be kept in mind when reading him: "*The meaning in history lies always in the present,* and when the present is conceived as the eschatological present by Christian faith the meaning in history is realized."[14] He goes on to say, "Do not look around yourself into universal history, you must look into your own personal history. Always in your present lies the meaning of history.... In every moment slumbers the possibility of being the eschatological moment. You must awaken it."[15] The special character of the Christian faith is that it provides the free gift of freedom which one needs in order to maintain oneself effectively in history. To say it in a few words, Bultmann is rescuing history, or at least the meaning in history, from the shadows of the past and placing it in the sunlight of the present. We recognize immediately the existentialist philosophy (as distinguished from existential faith) which lies behind this postulate, but that is not what primarily concerns us at this moment. Availing ourselves of the words of Karl Barth, "My present purpose is, then, not to speak for him, nor even, strictly speaking, against him, but, if I may put it thus, alongside of or around him."[16]

We are here primarily concerned with our own attempt to understand him. Questions or dissatisfactions must be postponed until this first attempt has been made. We must seek the answer to *why* as well as *how* Bultmann uses the categories of existentialist philosophy. It is insufficient to say that existentialist philosophy is the most adequate for dealing with the problem of history as it relates to the New Testament; we must also know why it is deemed most adequate. Bultmann himself provides an answer to this query in the essay "Bultmann Replies to His Critics."[17] He asserts, "In the first place, it is important to remember that every interpretation [of the New Testament] is actuated by the framing of specific questions, and without this there could be no interpretation at all."[18] Every interpreter approaches the New Testament with a *Vorverständnis* (preunderstanding), and the problems confronted in valid exegesis are, for Bultmann, part and parcel of the problem of history, for the clue to the meaning of history is to be found in the interpreter. Thus the problem of history leads necessarily to the problem of being an individual interpreter and can be clarified only from this vantage point.

This does *not* mean that history—or, more correctly, the texts that bear witness to history—imposes an existential model and that history must be judged in terms of this model.[19] Bultmann recognizes that this could require the surrender of history to subjectivism, but the meaning is not entirely subjective. What he wishes to determine is the condition under which an objective historical understanding is possible. This condition, he maintains, is the bearing of the interpreter's life on the matter in the text being examined. This "preunderstanding" which the interpreter brings "necessarily and unavoidably" to her encounter with history does not need to be explicit. It is *de facto* inherent in the person, inasmuch as she is not just a thing or an animal. "Man is not just something that happens in the world and in time, but is always aware of himself and concerned about himself." Bultmann's concept of humanity in relating to history will not allow human existence to be objectively perceived and subsumed under the law of causality. Rather, the nature of humanity consists in the fact that, "regardless of how clearly or dimly he knows himself," every person "has had to take charge of his own being and thus is responsible for himself." For this very reason the law of causality in history is not adequate for the nature of history as "the field of human decisions."[20]

On the basis of our knowledge of Bultmann's existentialist concept of history plus his primary hermeneutical principle of "preunderstanding," providing an answer to the "why" question we posed above, we can now proceed to the "how" of Bultmann's theology, namely, his program of demythologizing the New Testament.[21] What is mythology, and what is the purpose of myth as Bultmann sees it in the New Testament? "Mythology is the use of imagery to express the other worldly in terms of this world and the divine in terms of human life, the other side in terms of this side" (p. 10, note 2). "The real purpose of myth is not to present an objective picture of the world as it is, but to express man's understanding of himself in the world in which he lives.... Myth is an expression of man's conviction that the origin and purpose of the world in which he lives are to be sought not within it but beyond it" (p. 10). "Myth is also an expression of man's awareness that he is not lord of his own being ... myth expresses man's belief that in this state of dependence he can be delivered from the forces within the visible world.... The real purpose of myth is to speak of a transcendent power which controls the world and man, but that purpose is impeded and obscured by the terms in which it is expressed." From this Bultmann concludes that "myth contains elements which demand its own criticism—namely, its imagery with its apparent claim to objective validity" (p. 11).

As readily seen from the brief sketch of his concept of history and principle of hermeneutics above, this "objective validity" of myth cannot be allowed to stand; therefore, Bultmann can conclude: "Hence the importance of the New Testament mythology lies not in its imagery but in the understanding of existence which it enshrines" (p. 11). In order to determine whether this understanding of existence is true, we must do precisely what the "New Testament itself invites," namely, demythologize. In its broadest sense, demythologization is the interpretation of the New Testament in terms that contemporary persons can comprehend. In the specific way which Bultmann uses the term, it is a method of interpreting the mythological understanding of humanity held by the New Testament so that it becomes comprehensible to its hearer and compels one to make a decision "for oneself" with regard to the proclamation that has been heard.[22]

The New Testament speaks from within the world picture of the first-century Hellenistic Orient, especially in its recurrent use of the mythological "Jewish apocalyptic and Gnostic redemption myths" (p. 15). This is a mythology which modern man has left behind as obsolete (cf. pp. 3-6). Whereas angels, miracles, demons, spirits, and the rest were inextricably interwoven in the mind of first-century persons, modern science has washed our minds of the dirt of this superstition. Any type of literal acceptance of these concepts must be done away with. The proclamation of the gospel *in* the New Testament does not require, indeed it excludes, the proclamation of the worldview of the New Testament writers (p. 7). The faith of the New Testament must never be confused with the worldview of the New Testament.

But as steadfastly as Bultmann opposes literalism, just as adamantly does he reject liberalism. Focusing his criticism on Adolf von Harnack, he complains that liberalism, in direct opposition to fundamentalistic literalism, sought to entirely eliminate the mythology, thereby throwing out the baby with the bathwater (pp. 13-14). Because Bultmann's categories of reference are so different from traditional ones, he can easily be misunderstood at this point, and, indeed, has been. He is not seeking a reduction of the relevant material in the New Testament (p. 9), but he is asking for an "existentialist interpretation" (p. 16) of that material.

Having outlined what Bultmann does not do, we now proceed to the last step in our discussion of Bultmann, namely, what he does do in the process of demythologizing the New Testament. This revolves around two poles: (1) interpretation—which is the articulation of an ancient message in modern terminology; and (2) human existence—its potentiality and meaning. Demythologization is the interpretation of New Testament faith in terms of the understanding of human existence. It rests on exegesis, and therefore on the principles of hermeneutics, and the question it raises is: "What does New Testament faith say of human existence?"[23] Fundamentally the New Testament says, "This concerns you." If the New Testament is not *existential* ("existentialist"), then it is certainly *existentiell* ("existential"). The function of myth is to articulate the *existentiell* in a comprehensible way. This does not mean taking the mythological dynamic of the New Testament and turning it into a theological source book for dogma, for to Bultmann the decision of faith is not contingent "upon the accuracy of the biblical narrative—i.e., upon either the historical or the mythological aspects." Grace is to be found "in the Church's preaching of the Christ." In fact, unless we preach the biblical narrative as gospel, that is, preach it existentially to humanity in its sinful predicament, it is irrelevant.[24]

This brings us to the heart of the program of demythologization: the interpretation of the cross and the resurrection. The cross stands clearly as the twofold action of judgment and grace. It is judgment on sin and guilt, on the self-centeredness of humanity, but it is also the means of deliverance from sin and guilt. This is not the mythological past accomplishment of God; the cross is the confrontation of the hearer of the gospel with the demand that we accept this judgment and deliverance. The crucial point is not that it once took place, although few would deny that it did happen, but that when it did occur it inaugurated a new historic situation of judgment and redemption which in preaching, in sacraments, and in daily life continually challenges its hearers.[25]

The cross receives its validating significance through its immediate relatedness to the resurrection. The resurrection cannot be separated from the cross as if it were a "happy ending," a vindication of what seemed to be a tragic failure. If the power of the cross lies in its presenting us with our "death to the flesh" and "to the world," then the power of resurrection lies in its being our "new life" (Rom. 6:3-11). For Bultmann, we can safely say no more than this about resurrection. Historical research cannot establish the credibility of this event as it can the cross: "For the resurrection, of course, simply cannot be a visible fact in the realm of human history."[26] The only objective fact to which we can point is the church's proclamation of the risen Lord. For Bultmann, the church and its preaching are part of the resurrection; faith itself is the life of the resurrection, and the church stands on that new life as an article and ingredient of its faith.[27] The certainty of faith is not anchored to the events of the *past* but is founded in the *present* in which the listener is confronted with the proclamation of the cross: "Do not look around yourself into universal history, you must look into your own personal history. Always in your present lies the meaning in history. . . . In every moment slumbers the possibility of being the eschatological moment. You must awaken it."[28]

There are numerous questions which Bultmann leaves unanswered for us: If myth is the early church's interpretation of what may properly be called historic experience, what is the role and importance of the history which has been interpreted? Indeed, what is the history to which we must look for our comprehension of the New Testament mythology? For Bultmann, it can be reduced to two factors: the event of the cross and the church's reception of redemption. Yet he can say, "The word of God is not some mysterious oracle, but a sober, factual account of a human life, of Jesus of Nazareth, possessing saving efficacy for man."[29] The myth could not have arisen without history. Yet it is not the historical but the present proclamation that is determinative for Bultmann: "Jesus Christ is the eschatological event not as an established fact in past time but as repeatedly present, as addressing you and me here and now in preaching."[30] The awareness of being kerygmatically addressed determines our viewpoint of the historical material, but in what way? By what criterion do we say that the Jesus of history either is or is not the kerygma? Clearly, the New Testament writers were convinced that he was! The kerygma for them was not only the cross of Jesus, but also the resurrection of the Christ.

Barth and Bultmann make every effort to preserve the resurrection as an integral part of the gospel, albeit in completely different ways. Barth offers a history beyond historical reason and thereby neutralizes two hundred years of historical criticism. On the other hand, Bultmann makes place for the intellectual history of his theological forebears and reinterprets the Gospel texts as truth-bearing ideas, "myths" which are only at best partially rooted in actual historical events. The theology of these two giants towers above most other thinkers through the middle and into the third quarter of the twentieth century, and it is the theology of Bultmann which has had the most sustained influence with regard to the issues of resurrection and historical reason, especially in North America. In this connection there arises a New Quest for the Historical Jesus, followed by a specific group of scholars known as The Jesus Seminar. Although there are international scholars in both of these, we will pay particular attention to the North American contributions.

Chapter Three

Jesus in American Scholarship

The New Quest for the Historical Jesus

Whereas the theology of Rudolf Bultmann centered on the authentic life, a group of "neo-Bultmannian" scholars, led by Ernst Käsemann in 1953 with his lecture "The Problem of the Historical Jesus,"[1] revived the quest for the historical Jesus by placing Jesus' pre-Easter claim to authority at the center. The motif of the new quest no longer involves— as did the liberal quest for the historical Jesus—the *difference* between Jesus and the apostolic kerygma but involves precisely the *continuity* between the kerygma and Jesus himself. This insight is not really new with Bultmann's disciples but was basically expressed by him when he said, "Jesus' call to decision implies a christology... which will unfold the implications of the positive answer to his demand for the decision, the obedient response which acknowledges God's revelation in Jesus."[2] However, the use which the "neo-Bultmannians" made of this insight is one which Bultmann did not make. He did not consider a legitimation of the kerygma by a recourse to the historical Jesus to be necessary.[3] In an effort to allow history to play an important role again in theology, the disciples of Bultmann broke new ground. On the American theological scene, the professor of New Testament at Claremont School of Theology, James M. Robinson, was the primary spokesman for the "new quest." Using his 1959 contribution to the series *Studies in Biblical Theology* as our basic reference,[4] we will see why the new questers deem the original quest for the historical Jesus to be invalid and what they propose should take its place.

45

For the modern theologian it was no longer possible to use the term *historical Jesus* as an exact equivalent to *Jesus of Nazareth*. The adjective *historical* must be taken in a special technical sense which makes a "specific contribution to the total meaning of the expression" (p. 26). *Historical* is used in the sense of "things in the past which have been established by objective scholarship." Therefore, the expression *historical Jesus* means what we can know about Jesus of Nazareth "by means of the scientific methods of the historian" (p. 26).[6] Whereas "the nineteenth century saw the reality of the 'historical facts' in names, places, dates, occurrences, sequences, causes, effects," the modern historian views the essence of history as "the distinctively human, creative, unique, purposeful" intent in the events (p. 28). To replace the concept of history as being cold facts and data, Robinson proposes a new definition:

> The dimension in which man actually exists . . . the stance or outlook from which he acts, his understanding of his existence behind what he does, the way he meets his basic problems and the answer his life implies to the human dilemma, the significance he had as the environment of those who knew him, the continuing history his life produces, the possibility of existence which his life presents to me as an alternative—such matters as these have become central in an attempt to understand history. (pp. 28-29)

This existential element in man's life was left untouched by the original "questers" in their reconstruction of the life of Jesus. But there is more to the fallacy of the original quest than the definition of history, and to these points also Robinson turns his attention.

The basis on which the nineteenth-century theologians wished to build their life of Jesus consisted of viewing the New Testament sources as "objective, positivistic historiography." This foundation is now seen as invalid by the twentieth-century historian, who recognizes that "the Gospels are the devotional literature of the primitive Church, rather than the products of scholarship" (p. 35). This basic reorientation is to the effect that "*all* the tradition about Jesus survived only in so far as it served some function in the life and worship of the primitive Church. History survived only as *kerygma*" (p. 37).

In much the same way as the positivistic understanding of history gave way to an understanding centering in the intentions and concepts of existence, so also has historical methodology shifted from a primary concern for recording the past "as it actually was" to seeing the historian's task as consisting of "understanding those deep-lying intentions of the past, by involving one's selfhood in an encounter in which one's own intentions and views of existence are put in question, and perhaps altered or even radically reversed. Now the *kerygma* is formally analogous to this new approach to the historian's task, for it consists in an initial understanding of the deeper meaning of Jesus" (p. 39).

This is the point at which Robinson begins to break some new ground for the role of history in theologizing. His rejection of positivistic history and the acceptance of an existential, kerygmatic history leads him to draw the conclusion that "the introduction of details into the 'historical section of the kerygma' is valid only as an impressive way of witnessing to this kerygmatic message, that in suffering lies glory, in death resides life, [and] in judgement is to be found grace" (p. 52).[7] These paradoxical truths are the essential and creative elements of humanity, whose reality "would not *be* apart from the event" in which they occur. Their truth cannot be known by "Platonic recollection or inference from a rational principle, but only through historical encounter" (p. 67). As we have already noted above, history is the act of intention, the commitment, the meaning of intention, behind the external occurrence. When we go behind the external "acts of self-actualization," we discover the real self of the actor. It is the task of the modern historian to grasp such acts of intention and thereby "lay hold of the selfhood which is therein revealed" (p. 68).

Robinson explains that "the self is not simply one's personality" as it has been formed by "influences and ingredients present in one's heritage and development. Rather selfhood is constituted by commitment to a context, from which commitment one's existence arises." Our empirical *habitus* is not identical with the self, but it is "the inescapable medium through which the self expresses itself." It is a drastic mistake to assume that selfhood can be described in terms of "causal relationships and cultural ingredients." This would be a psychological description of personality makeup. This, of course, plays a role, but selfhood is more: "Selfhood results from implicit or explicit commitment to a kind of existence, and is to be understood only in terms of that commitment, i.e., by laying hold of the understanding of existence in terms of which the self is constituted" (p. 68).

It is now clear to us why and how Robinson is not proposing a *Historie* of the life of Jesus but a *Geschichte* of Jesus (p. 71). It is not considered a problem that the "chronology and causalities for the public ministry are gone" (p. 69). In the various documents of the New Testament, we are provided with "sufficient insight into Jesus' intention to encounter his historical action, and enough insight into the understanding of existence presupposed in his intention to encounter his selfhood...consequently Jesus' history and selfhood *are* accessible to modern historiography and biography" (p. 70).

The "new questers" have not attempted to invalidate the significance of the cross or its proclamation, the kerygma, but rather have taken a step, considered unnecessary by Bultmann, to certify the validity of the cross and the kerygma by returning to the life of the historical Jesus and finding the real significance of that life in an existential concept of the self. Theirs is not an attempt to "prove" the cross and the kerygma but an attempt to establish the continuity of the Jesus of history with the Christ of faith, and thus, in one mighty sweep, remove the elements of skepticism which remained with Barth and Bultmann. This question is, Have they succeeded?

There can be no doubt that the stress on "intentions, stances and concepts of existence" (p. 39) made by Robinson is a much needed emphasis that rescues history from drying up into the chronicling of dusty, antiquated data. He reminds us that human action is finally intelligible only as a quest for meaning. It seems, however, that it is at his point of greatest strength that Robinson is also at his weakest. Historical judgments about the *meaning* behind an event are the type of judgments which logically and epistemologically can least support the argument. It would seem that the extraction of the self-concept of Jesus would have to be done on the basis of inferences drawn from the so-called external data of chronology and events, things which we do not really *need,* according to Robinson. The monolithic view of history founded in "meaning" and disregarding chronology proposed by Robinson leaves a number of questions unanswered, not the least important of which is the one Bultmann himself noted: "The greatest embarrassment to the attempt to reconstruct a portrait of Jesus is the fact that we cannot know how Jesus understood his end, his death."[8] In the face of this, the believer is left still with an intellectual and moral dilemma: How does what one believes religiously (in search of ultimate meaning) affect what one can know rationally; and if belief affects knowledge, is this permissible?

The Morality of Historical Reason as Knowledge

In the late 1960s a book appeared that summarized these ethical and theological implications, Van Harvey's *The Historian and the Believer*. Harvey begins a chapter in his book with a story that is still pertinent to theology today, especially as it relates to our confidence to proclaim as part of the gospel story the assertion that God raised Christ. The title of Harvey's chapter is "The Morality of Historical Knowledge and Traditional Belief." Along with Harvey's comments, this is the story:[9]

> About the turn of the century, the evangelical theologian Martin Kähler related this experience:
>
> A young man from a long believing home came to me deeply moved inwardly and unsatisfied with modern rationalism. In a discussion with [Professor] Tholuck, he had been told that if it could be demonstrated that the Fourth Gospel had not been written by John the son of Zebedee, then Christendom would have suffered a blow from which it would be very difficult to survive. This judgment profoundly shook the youth. The clarity with which I might have helped him through the matter escaped me at that time, and he climbed from that point on down the ladder of doubt.... That which caused him to stumble in his quest for a firm foundation was the linking of certainty, so far as Christian conviction is concerned, with the results of historical criticism of the sources, results that cannot be anticipated in advance. He was skeptical of all so-called positive results, which is to say, results favorable to the tradition, because he was troubled by the falsifying influence of the demand for belief lying behind them. Tholuck could hardly have calculated the magnitude of his utterance. Since that time it has become progressively more certain to me that my Christian conviction can have no causal connection with the "genuineness" the Gospels may have.

With this story in a footnote of the early pages of his book on the historical Jesus that we discussed earlier, Kähler proceeds to define a different basis for belief. About this entire phenomenon, Harvey comments:

> This story reveals a great deal concerning the pathos of the modern mind. The pathos does not consist primarily in the conflict between the student's craving for certainty and his realization that historical inquiry could never, in the nature of the case, gratify it. It consists, rather, in his awareness of the falsifying influence belief frequently exercises on critical judgment, so that he is most distrustful of just those answers he would most like to believe [Italics added]. Indeed, it is just because he is aware that he would like to believe them that he distrusts any tendency in himself to do so.
>
> This pathos is intelligible only if we realize that the revolution in consciousness, which came about with the emergence of historical thinking, is fundamentally a revolution in the morality of knowledge...[but this revolution] occurred only when integrity was identified with loyalty to the methodological procedures of the intellectual community, when historians agreed on general canons of inquiry....The problem of faith and history is not merely a problem of two logics or two methodologies. It is a problem, as Kähler's story reveals, of two ethics of judgment. Otherwise, it is impossible to account for the fierce sense of honesty, the suspicion of one's desire to believe, the sense of resentment against obscurantism, which underlie so much unbelief. Furthermore, only in this way is it possible to account for the character of much Protestant theology in the last century, because a great deal of that theology, as the closing sentences of Martin Kähler's story reveal, is an attempt so to formulate the faith that it escapes the accusation of being intellectually irresponsible. From liberal Protestantism to the new hermeneutic, Protestant theology may be regarded as a series of salvage operations, attempts to show how one can still believe in Jesus Christ and not violate an ideal of intellectual integrity.

Inherent in this perspective is the assumption that the individual may not be deeply invested personally in the issues at stake; or if she is, that vesting must be set aside for the sake of disinterested objectivity.

If you compare the preface to the first edition of Harvey's work in 1965 with the paperback in 1968, you will notice what seems at first glance to be a trivial difference. The first preface was penned in Dallas while Harvey was professor of theology and director of the Graduate Program in Theology at the Perkins School of Theology, Southern Methodist University. The second preface was penned at the University of Pennsylvania where Harvey had become "Professor of Religious Thought." Not least in his decision to leave Perkins (and his post teaching theology and training ministers) was the crisis of conscience he experienced regarding the conflict between traditional belief and the morality of historical knowledge. Harvey came to the conclusion that the historic Christian faith is not intellectually tenable and that for him to continue to teach in a seminary setting was less than honest. As a result of this conviction, he moved to a religious studies program.

To be sure the shadow of the Enlightenment is long, and its implications for the church and the theological education of its ministry is profound. Some choose to leave this arena, others choose to stay, realizing full well the challenges. Is it the case that we in the '90s have moved far beyond these fundamental issues and concepts that largely defined theological conversation for nearly three hundred years and were still so influential thirty years ago? If these are "modern questions" and we are "postmodern," then we should be well beyond the morality of knowledge issue that was so significant for Harvey. To be sure, some scholars have moved on, but certainly not all. It is difficult to believe we are really postmodern with regard to the historic affirmations of gospel, resurrection, and personal redemption. If we were, then there would be little or no interest in the Dutch blockbuster by Harry Kuitert, *Het Algemeen Betwijfeld Christijlek Geloof (The Widely Doubted Christian Faith)*,[10] which went through *twelve* Dutch printings in 1992, its first year off the press, with continued reprintings since. In the same vein are *Zeker Weten (Certain Knowledge, 1994)*[11] which has gone through seven printings, and *Jezus: nalatenschap van het Christendom* (1998).[12] On the scene in Germany is Gerd Lüdemann's bestseller, *Die Auferstehung Jesu,*[13] accompanied by explosions of chagrin, amusement, and outrage in the popular press. Even as I prepared the final draft of this manuscript, I learned that Professor Lüdemann has, in fact, renounced Christianity. In an interview at the University of Göttingen, where he has served as Professor of New Testament Studies since 1983, Lüdemann told *Idea*, the information service of the German Evangelical Alliance: *I no longer describe myself as a Christian.* This statement was made in discussion of his latest book about Jesus, in which he calls the biblical witness to Jesus "the great deception." He had earlier described ordination to Christian ministry on the basis of the Bible and the creeds as "schizophrenia." He asserts that anyone who takes Christian doctrine seriously is a "Fundamentalist," but that "liberal theologians" *reinterpret* Christian doctrine in such a way that they may continue to describe themselves, in good conscience, as Christian—a practice Lüdemann describes as "contemptible."[14]

On the American scene we have the continuing saga of the thoroughly modern rhetoric and historicist methodology of the Jesus Seminar personalities, from the more restrained Marcus Borg to the most "thoroughly modern Millie" of them all, Bishop John Shelby Spong, a marvelous example of the "liberal" referred to by Lüdemann. It is to the Jesus Seminar and these two personalities that we devote our attention in the closing pages of this chapter. As we recount the perspective of these two authors, we will also engage them by asking questions and pointing to areas in which their points seem less than adequate.

The Jesus Seminar

The earliest significant full-scale publication of this group came in 1993, *The Five Gospels.* The title itself was an attention-getter in that it openly called into question the traditional teaching that there are *four* Gospels, the fifth now being *The Gospel of Thomas,* found in 1945 in the "Gnostic library" of Nag Hammadi. The place of *Thomas* in the Jesus Seminar's frame of reference is pivotal. The importance attached to it paves the way to comprehensively rethinking the history of Jesus.

From its first publication at the end of the 1950s, scholars have steadily pushed back *Thomas's* proposed date of origin. Early dating had suggested a time in the third or fourth century; however, as the opinion gained ground that the Gnostic influence was not as great as had been originally supposed the date was pushed back, eventually to the first half of the second century, around 140 C.E. Meanwhile it became clear that the *Gospel of Thomas* is composed of different layers—containing "Gnostic sayings" but also composition clearly uninfluenced by Gnosticism. James Robinson, an early member of the Jesus Seminar whose thought we examined earlier, became convinced that *Thomas* was important for the study of the historical Jesus,[15] and others were convinced that it was a fifth independent source which should take its place alongside the canonical Gospels in the New Testament.[16] If this conclusion is to be final, an early dating of *Thomas* is required, and some scholars placed the nucleus of the composition as early as between 50 and 60 C.E.[17] The results of the Jesus Seminar with regard to the canonical Gospel affirmations of the resurrection reflect these developments in Jesus studies and the consequent importance allotted to the *Gospel of Thomas*. This composition contains only "sayings" of Jesus. Narrative is absent. There are no miracle stories, nor are there any stories about his passion and death. There is not a word about Jesus' death on the cross in any of its 114 sayings. When suppositions allow that these sayings represent an early stage of church tradition about Jesus, some scholars have concluded that this is a form of very early christological reflection on the part of the church. In contrast to the letters of the apostle Paul, the cross does not have a central place and the resurrection has no place at all. Consonant with this, one reads *Thomas*'s "sayings" and finds few christological titles. Nowhere is Jesus called Messiah or Christ, nor is his name connected with the titles *Lord* or *Son of man*. Jesus is fundamentally a Jewish wisdom teacher with his eye fixed only on the present. Eschatology and the future are absent.

From this frame of reference, it is logical that Jesus Seminar participants can restructure their vision of Jesus in radical opposition to the traditional canonical view in which teaching-life-death-resurrection are constituent parts of a composite view. Such is the case with Bishop John Shelby Spong as well as Professor Marcus Borg, but the intention and tone of the two in their writings is quite different. Whereas Borg is reasoned and reasonable, Bishop Spong clearly aims for the headlines, for his broad and sweeping assertions border on the sensational. In this Episcopal bishop's first publishing venture in Jesus studies, *Born of a Woman*, Spong moves from the rather commonplace observation that the infancy accounts about Jesus are historically late compositions to his fabricated assertion that Mary was actually raped as a teenager (asserted also by Lüdemann) and taken under the protective wing of Joseph when she was found to be pregnant.[18] In his desire to free us from literal readings of the Christian Scriptures that purport to be related to history, he is himself free to construct scenarios that are more believable to the modern reader. Whether there is good historical warrant beyond contemporary structures of credibility for believing his sensational fabrications does not seem to be part of the bishop's perspective. As Luke Johnson has observed, "Spong is not so much interested . . . in what 'really happened' as he is in freeing Christianity from its dogmatic entanglements, which he more or less identifies with fundamentalism."[19] Johnson may be correct that Spong is not concerned with what really happened, but this does not prevent the bishop from speculating about what might have happened. This is nowhere more evident than in Spong's handling of the traditional Christian affirmation of the resurrection of Jesus. His rationale is that the church got both the birth story and the Easter story "all wrong."[20]

Bishop Spong is quite forthright that his perspective on the resurrection arose in a highly personal manner and that his emerging perspective is unfriendly to traditional versions of Christianity: "Slowly, ever so slowly, but equally ever so surely, a separation began to occur for me between the experience captured for us Christians in the word *Easter* and the interpretation of that experience found in both the Christian Scriptures and the developing Christian traditions, which have borrowed freely, *if not always consciously* [emphasis mine], from the mythology of the ages." This supposed realization frees Spong to approach resurrection from a "new perspective," but he remains insistent that this move is made with a "deep conviction that my understanding of Christianity is rooted firmly in the reality of Easter." He "insist[s] that Easter [should not] be understood as an objective supernatural event that occurred inside human history. I do maintain that the effects of that experience called Easter are demonstrably objective," and that "Jesus, in the experience called Easter, transcended the limits of human finitude expressed in the ultimate symbol of that finitude—death. I do believe that those of us who are called by this Jesus to live in him and in the Spirit that he made available to us will also transcend that final barrier [death]. Furthermore I believe that what we Christians call heaven is in fact real" (pp. xi-xii).

What we have here is a selective option for supernatural. The very word *supernatural* is problematic, but let us agree that it means "more than that which can be explained entirely by historical reason and logic." Spong asserts that we may deselect resurrection as event, but we choose to affirm life after physical death. We affirm the concept of transcendent reality, and we even grant reality status to heaven. It is proper to assume that these happen to us in a real way, a way that is more than the projection of our imagination, but it is not proper to assume that resurrection actually happened to Jesus. In some way or another, resurrection will happen to us, even if resurrection did not happen to Jesus. Just how Spong works his way into this set of assertions is very interesting, and in order to understand it well, we must be aware that his fundamental hermeneutic for the Jesus stories revolves around the Jewish concept *midrash*.

Midrash is both a collection of the interpretations of sacred Scripture and a method for the continued expansion of the sacred Scripture. It comes in three forms: Halakah, Haggadah, and Pesiqta. Halakah is an interpretation of the sacred Torah. Haggadah is the interpretation of a story or an event by relating it to another story or event in sacred history. Pesiqta is a whole sermon or an exhortation written midrashically to capture themes of the past to enable them to be perceived as operative in the present. According to Spong, "The sermons of Peter and Paul in the Book of Acts, as well as the long speech of Stephen, are examples in the New Testament of Pesiqta" (p. 8). It is important at this juncture to note the formal definition that S. Aarowitz in *The Jewish Encyclopedia* assigns to *midrash*: "The attempt to penetrate into the spirit of the text, to examine the text from all sides, to derive interpretations not immediately obvious, to illumine the future by appealing to the past."[21] We note in this formal definition that the factuality of events appealed to in the past is not an issue. Although Spong refers to this definition, he uses *midrash* in a manner that goes far beyond the parameters set out in the article by Aarowitz. The use of various forms of midrash in both the Old and New Testaments is widely recognized, but the manner in which Spong interprets the use of midrash and the manner in which he engages in his own midrashic interpretations and reconstructions of the New Testament is unusual indeed.

Bishop Spong believes that early Christianity forgot its Jewish roots, and in a fit of anti-Semitism substituted a crude literalism for midrash as its interpretive grid for the first-century Christian documents. Since, according to Spong, virtually all of the Jesus narratives are midrash, even consciously mythological, and unconnected to actual past events, "The question to ask of this midrash tradition is not, Did it really happen? That is a Western question tied to a Western mind-set that seeks . . . to measure and describe those things defined as objectively real" (pp. 9-10). This is an example of "asking the wrong questions of a tradition that employs midrash to tell its story" (p. 11). We will sort some of this out at the end of the chapter, but Spong does not have it quite right here. Western rationalism since the Enlightenment has been preoccupied with two issues historically: *whether* an event happened and *how* an event happened. Clearly midrash as a vehicle for teaching truth matured in its form and application long before and in another cultural setting than the canons of historical criticism. It does not follow, however, that the Jewish Rabbis were not concerned, for example, with whether the Exodus happened, or whether there was an actual Egyptian or Babylonian captivity. Avoiding an unhealthy *preoccupation* with whether purported events fit the canons of historical reason is not the same as assuming that purported events could not have happened because they do not fit modernist assumptions. Fortunately the Rabbinic and New Testament traditions were not encumbered with these assumptions (although Spong is), and the use of midrash by them does not imply that the events being interpreted didactically to the faith community never did happen, nor does the use of midrash necessarily imply that it is inconsequential whether any of the events actually took place.

Because Spong's historicist assumptions disallow that certain events took place, he must either find an existential meaning in the original stories or he must invent a narrative more plausible to modernist assumptions. The bishop does both. Historical assumptions drive Spong to this necessity because he is convinced that the New Testament accounts are neither sufficiently coherent nor do they correspond adequately to the way things could have happened. Both of these assumptions, coherence and correspondence, are also Western in their application, but Spong uses them nevertheless. He uses them first to discount the canonical accounts: "I believe that there can be a new scenario for a

Christian future. . . . It cannot begin, however, with a literal biblical text that describes either the birth of the transcendent reality found in Jesus of Nazareth or in the rebirth of that transcendent reality in the moment called resurrection" (p. 19). Spong takes the midrashic category of "timelessness" (i.e., that the interpreter is teaching a truth that is not bound by time) and superimposes it upon the entire resurrection story: "It is layer after layer of timelessness. Every reference to Jesus going up to Jerusalem, every mention of three days . . . every account of the rebuilding of the temple—these are but midrashic traditions that seek to communicate the meaning of Easter. . . . Midrash means that when one enters the Scriptures, one must abandon linear time" (p. 20). It is an interesting move to assert that since "three days" is midrash, the event itself did not actually happen. He continues, "Easter has nothing to do with angelic announcements or empty tombs. It has nothing to do with time periods. . . . It has nothing to do with resuscitated bodies that appear and disappear or that finally exit this world in a heavenly ascension. Those are but the human, midrashic vehicles employed to carry the transcendent meaning of Easter by those who must speak of the unspeakable and describe the indescribable because the power of the *event* [emphasis mine] was undeniably real" (p. 21).

Although he uses the word *event*, Spong really means *experience of Easter.* There is no resurrection event, but there is an Easter event: "I believe that this experience is both real and true but that the details that describe it cannot be literalized." There is religious truth inherent in the Easter experience, but there is no historical event of resurrection. It is religiously true but not historically factual. Resurrection is, nonetheless, experienced. It is key, for Spong asserts that there is

> a presence I call God. . . . My access to that presence is through a life referred to in history as Jesus of Nazareth but called, by faith and in the language of midrash and mythology, the Christ of God. . . . I believe that those of us who have found our lives inside his life can also make that journey and can know this Christ as our way, our truth, and our life, through whom we too can approach the presence of God, and . . . know the timelessness of eternity. Yes, I even mean to state that I believe that this life I have in this Christ is beyond the power of death to extinguish or even to diminish. (p. 21)

It is an interesting mix of objectivity and subjectivity that we see at work here. On the one hand, we encounter the axiomatic assumption "The dawn of Christianity was connected with the life of one known as Jesus of Nazareth. But there are almost no objective records anywhere that can verify a single fact of his life. There are only things called Christian Scriptures, written by passionate believers, through which we can gain access to this man's life" (p. 24). These writings cannot be accepted as accurate because they are written by passionate believers, but we have a Bishop of the church, clearly passionate to make his religious viewpoint credible, claiming truth status for beliefs that are completely beyond verification: life beyond death and heaven. The essence of his logic is this: The canonical Gospels and epistles are not objective, but the truth they both assume and describe is an objective referent about which a coherent midrash can be composed, a midrash that corresponds to reality. Although we do not really have good clues about what happened, since the reporters are believers and therefore biased, we believe that they were telling us about true transcendence even if they were not giving us good historical information. Once again, we have an admixture of subjectivity with objectivity. We do not know what happened, but we can know the truth behind the stories about events that did not occur.

This is not as nonsensical as it sounds when we keep in view the canons of historical reason which dictate the realm of possibilities for Spong: An event cannot be historically true if we cannot define empirically its causality. For every effect there must be a rationally defined cause. If one does not know the correlation between these two, one does not actually *know* anything. Second, there is the principle of criticism, by which is meant that our judgments about the past are made only in degrees of plausibility or probability; and finally, the principle of analogy requires that we are able to make judgments of probability only if our own present experience is not radically dissimilar to the events or experiences others purport to be actual. Within this thoroughly rationalist set of assumptions bequeathed to us at the end of the nineteenth century, Spong is certain what is not accurate in the canonical accounts: "It is easy to identify the legendary elements of the resurrection narratives. Angels who descend in earthquakes, speak, and roll back stones; tombs that are empty; apparitions that appear and disappear; rich men who make graves available; thieves who comment from their crosses of pain—these are the legends all. Sacred legends, . . . but legends nonetheless" (p. 233). And he drives his point home, "To press this even further, . . . all of the appearance narratives that purport to be the physical manifestations of the dead body that somehow was enabled to be revivified and to walk out of a tomb are also legends and myths. . . . Thomas did not touch the physical wounds. Resurrection may mean many things, but these details are not literally a part of that reality" (pp. 235-36).

This set of assumptions and assertions leaves the reader with a very important fundamental question: What then did happen? And Spong's answer is clear: "Let me first state the obvious: No one can finally do anything other than speculate!" (p. 237). And speculate he does, with his own imaginative account done within the canons of criticism. And then we have a curious appeal for granting credibility to his plausible construction, a chapter entitled, "Grounding the Speculation in Scripture." He does not tell the reader why he feels this is necessary, but we may assume that it is because the Bishop is not willing to cut himself off completely from the canonical writings. He also wants to believe in the "truth behind the resurrection," even if he denies that an actual resurrection took place. The manner in which he constructs his story of how the "resurrection may have happened" is interesting reading and important to our story:

One of the three great pilgrim feasts of the Jewish people in the first century C.E. was the festival of Tabernacles. Most Jews of that era in fact deemed this celebration to be the greatest, the most welcome, and the most fun. Tabernacles had many themes. It was a harvest feast to give thanks for the bounty of the earth, not dissimilar from the American celebration of Thanksgiving. But it was also a time to pray for rain, to acknowledge the light of God, and to remember the wilderness wandering era of Jewish history. Tabernacles also came in the same month as Rosh Hashanah, the Jewish New Year, and Yom Kippur, the solemn Day of Atonement. The contrast with these more somber liturgical traditions only acted to heighten the sense of joy and happiness that marked the festival of Tabernacles. . . .

Peter, having had in Galilee an experience of the inbreaking reality of God that he called resurrection, which included seeing

Jesus of Nazareth as part of who God was and is, shared that experience first with his Galilean fishing partners James, John, and, maybe, Andrew. It was electrifying, and, though not clear to any of them, it was real. It had come in a combination of signs, grief, inner conflict, and the sacramental act of breaking bread and seeing through that symbol the body of Jesus broken on the cross as the ultimate sign of the infinite love of God. This compelled Peter and the Galilean group to go up to Jerusalem for the feast of Tabernacles, a journey that John placed into the historic life of Jesus, but he preserved the original, nonhistorical, context by writing the narrative in such a way as to be read on two levels at once. The synoptic writers, by contrast, simply attached to Jesus' final journey to Jerusalem, at the time of the Passover when the crucifixion occurred, all of the symbols of the later journey during Tabernacles. In fact, however, this journey to Jerusalem for the feast of Tabernacles took place, I now propose, some six months after the crucifixion and was led by Peter, not Jesus. But it was a Peter who believed himself to be carrying the undeniable message of his Lord risen and living to those in Jerusalem who had not yet seen the Lord risen and enthroned in heaven.

Sharing the story of what Peter called "the appearance of Jesus resurrected into the very presence of God" with his Jerusalem friends in the context of Tabernacles gave the whole experience a new and vital frame of reference. The newly gathered community of believers now joined the processions around the altar, waving their branches of palms and other greenery. They shouted their hosannahs and their liturgical refrain "Blessed is he who comes in the name of the Lord." They built a sukkoth, or temporary shelter, that was later, I believe, incorporated into the Christian story as the temporary tomb in Joseph's lonely garden. They went to the sukkoth carrying the box called an ethrog, containing the fragrant citron fruit and blossom, which I am now convinced got incorporated into the later resurrection narratives as the spices carried by the women, but for a purpose that never was really clear. As the liturgy of Tabernacles developed under the impact of this Christian revelation, it included a procession to a tomb-like temporary dwelling, where one member of the community would dress in white to announce, as part of the liturgy, "He is not here, behold, the place where they laid him." In time that white-robed liturgical functionary was transformed by Gospel writers into the eschatological angel or angels who announced to the women the resurrection message that the tomb, which was a symbol of death, could not contain Jesus of Nazareth.

But above all else, I believe it was the ceremonial meal that was required to be eaten in the sukkoth that bound together forever the experience of the risen Lord and the reenactment of the common meal in which bread was broken and wine was poured. In that sacramental act eyes were opened to see the body of Jesus as the bread of life, broken for the world to feed the deepest human hunger for God, and hearts were opened by the blood of Jesus, understood as the atoning sacrifice that lifted human beings anew into God's presence. . . .

The resurrection thus began with Peter, who finally understood that it was the duty of those who loved Christ to feed the sheep of Christ, but it soon journeyed to Jerusalem and found expression inside the Jewish festival of Tabernacles. That festival, lost by and large to the gentile consciousness after the fall of Jerusalem, was preserved in a single reference in John 7, but it was incorporated into the passion narratives by moving all of the symbols of Tabernacles into the dominant celebration of Passover. (pp. 261, 277-78)

Spong's final point is that when Peter and the other Galilean disciples took their faith to Jerusalem during the feast of the Tabernacles, some six months after the death of Jesus, theirs was the real triumphal entry, the original Palm Sunday. In time the Jerusalem setting for the resurrection became the primary one, and the Jerusalem Easter tradition is actually a part of the celebration of Tabernacles. The Christian church's great failing is that we are ignorant of midrash, and in this bliss we interpret the biblical narratives as if they corresponded to actual events. Spong concludes: "The Jerusalem Easter legends are not to be dismissed as untrue. They are meant to be probed for clues, as I trust I have done adequately. Behind the legends . . . there is a reality I can never deny. Jesus lives. I have seen the Lord" (p. 282). It seems that what Spong offers the church is *a* resurrection without *the* resurrection. The intellectual criteria that define knowledge will not allow actual resurrection, so he has to opt for an existential resurrection. On this point Bishop Spong is consistent, and a superlative representative of one who remains thoroughly "modern" in an era called "postmodern."

When we turn to professor Marcus Borg, Hundere Distinguished Professor at Oregon State University, we encounter scholarship that is much less characterized by the spectacular, although he does work within the historicist parameters set out by the Jesus Seminar. Among his several writings pertinent to our story are: *Jesus: A New Vision* (1987); *Meeting Jesus Again for the First Time* (1994); *Jesus in Contemporary Scholarship* (1994); and *The God We Never Knew* (1997). It is important to know that Borg is a confessing Christian who understands himself to be on an intellectual journey in which Jesus Seminar research has helped him to be more truly Christian in his beliefs. He affirms, "I grew up with God. . . . The subject and question of God—devotionally, intellectually, and experientially—has been central. I have been praising God, thinking about God, and yearning for God all of my life." His intellectual dilemma is, however, best characterized by the sentence that opens the paragraph from which we are quoting, "I am a Jesus scholar and not a God scholar." By this Borg means that he is not a specialist in doctrine of God subjects, but he adds, "As a Jesus scholar I have found it impossible to say very much about Jesus without also talking about God." He then concludes, "Finally, my own Christian journey (from initial belief through doubt and unbelief to rediscovery and reformulation) has centered on the question of God."[22]

In our consideration of scholarly opinion on the resurrection to this point, there has been an unspoken assumption about this Jesus-God issue to which Borg alerts us, namely, historic Christian affirmations about Jesus' resurrection assume that God raised Jesus. It is also assumed that this resurrection is the continuation of a unique relationship intrinsic to God's very being and to Jesus' unique being. To talk about Jesus is to talk about God. Although Borg has very carefully chosen his words on this topic, it is clear that a fundamental part of his intellectual journey is related to the salvific "being" of Jesus as well as to the historical being, Jesus. Expressed in question form, Does the historic person Jesus have any ultimate or final salvific meaning to humanity? Or, Can you separate a discussion of the historical Jesus from the consideration of the saving work of God in creation through Jesus? In his statements Borg does not seem to believe that you can separate these two in that he has "found it impossible to say very much about Jesus without also talking about God." It would seem, then, that there is an intrinsic connection between Jesus and God, and that there is also an intrinsic connection between historical issues pertaining to Jesus' existence and salvific issues related to Jesus' ultimate significance. And we are again right back in the middle of "the problem of the moral-ity of knowledge" that confounded historical scholars thirty years ago—the connection between belief and knowledge. Borg is a confessing Christian trying to work his way through the problem of historical verification to an intellectually viable theory of knowledge about God. Before we attempt our own "solution" to this dilemma, it is instructive for us to see how Borg addresses the issue.

Were this an open forum debate with Professor Borg, he would perhaps say that I have misunderstood his meaning. In another writing he asserts with regard to the connection between historic-ity and faith, "I agree in part with the position of Kähler and Schweitzer. . . . Namely . . . that historical knowledge of Jesus is not essential to being a Christian." For Borg, "This seems self-evidently true; if it were not, then we would have to say that the vast majority of Christians throughout the centuries have not had authentic faith, for there was no possibility of historical knowl-edge of Jesus until the birth of the quest a couple of centuries ago."[23] Notice the assumption that is at work here: Until the rise of modern historical scholarship governed by the canons of his-torical criticism, valid or accurate historical knowledge was by definition impossible. It is critical to underscore this fundamen-tally assumed perspective, for it shapes his entire working hypoth-esis about what one can or cannot know. If we follow the canons of historical criticism, we can *know* important information; if we do not have these canons at our disposal or if we choose not to abide by their restrictive canon, we cannot know this informa-tion. Since people who lived prior to the modern period did not have the canons of historical knowledge available to them, they did not have accurate historical knowledge. This being the case, and not wanting to assume that all prior generations were "faith-less," we must assume that there is no connection between his-torical knowledge and faith. At this juncture, a fine point of logic is in order. Borg is denying that there is a "necessary connection" between faith and historical knowledge; that is, that you must have the historical knowledge in order to have true faith. He does not qualify his assertion in this manner, but leaves the implica-tions to a much wider range, namely, that historical knowledge is irrelevant to faith.

To the question "What is this faith?" he gives an existential, pragmatic response: "In affirming that historical knowledge of Jesus is not essential for Christian faith, it is important to be precise about what one means by 'faith.' I am using 'faith' in a relatively narrow sense to refer to one's relationship to God, and Christian faith specifically is a trusting relationship to God as mediated by the Christian tradition. Faith in this sense—as one's relationship to God—is not dependent upon historical knowledge of Jesus." Borg follows this with a distinction between "the Christian tradition," that which mediates to the believer a trusting relationship with God—for which historical knowledge is irrelevant, and "the Christian faith," by which he means the historic totality of Christianity—for which "it seems obvious to me that historical knowledge of Jesus is relevant" (p. 193). Unfortunately, Borg has not gone further in sorting out for us the difference between "the Christian tradition" and "the Christian faith." What we seem to have is a distinction between what we *believe* (tradition) and what we *know* (Christian faith). The problem is immediately obvious when put this way: *The* Christian faith is related to knowing, but to *a* Christian's personal faith knowledge is irrelevant.

This is more than the splitting of logical hairs. This is a very practical issue, and of this Marcus Borg is very much aware: "Images of Jesus *in fact* very much affect images of the Christian life. Much of the scholarly debate about the significance of historical knowledge about Jesus for Christians has focused on the question of whether it *ought* to be significant" (p. 193). Borg believes that what we think of Jesus does matter, but he moves us away from the issue of "historical fact" to "images of Jesus." He is aware that he has not escaped the conundrum of fact versus true knowledge, but he shifts to metaphorical language in order to preserve the integrity of Christian affirmation.

There is first the "popular image...of Jesus as the divine savior." This gives "answers to the classic questions of Jesus' identity, mission, and message," by affirming "the saving purpose of his death, and the importance of believing in him." We saw above that Borg uses the language of "trusting" in reference to his own journey, but here he seems to shade this believing frame of reference in a rather negative light: "It creates what we might call a *fideistic* image of the Christian life, one whose essential quality is believing that Jesus is one's savior" (pp. 193-94). There is a second image that is not quite as widespread, that of Jesus as teacher. In popular form this is a "de-dogmatized image of Jesus," and it occurs most commonly when persons have lost confidence in the doctrinal features of the savior image. In the final analysis, this usually turns out to be little more than a moralistic understanding of the Christian life: "What remains is Jesus as a teacher of ethics or morals, and it leads to . . . [asserting that] the Christian life consists of 'being good' or of following 'the golden rule'" (p. 194). Borg touches on several other possible images of Jesus, but his point is clear: "The question is not so much *whether* images of Jesus *ought* to have theological significance. Rather, they *do* have theological significance at the very practical immediate level of Christian understanding, devotion, and piety. Our choice is to let that significance be largely unrecognized, unconscious, and unchallenged, or to be conscious and intentional about the relationship. In short, because historical scholarship about Jesus affects our image of Jesus and thus our image of the Christian life, it matters" (pp. 194-95).

It is clear that Borg sees himself as a missionary to an intellectual lost generation of people who can no longer accept historic Christian affirmations like resurrection, and within the parameters which he defines based on his presuppositions, his case is quite persuasive. There is, however, one caveat that he puts in a footnote which should not be overlooked, for it is the most critical concession that he makes in all of his writings on Jesus. With regard to the traditional Easter teaching that "God raise[d] the corpse of Jesus from the tomb," in the footnote he says, "Caution about the limits of our knowledge leads me to say that I cannot rule out that possibility. . . . It [the argument for the truth of the resurrection] begins with the claim that the Easter stories are factually true and then argues that you can therefore take God, Jesus, and Christianity seriously. But presumably taking God and Jesus seriously is the basis for being willing to take these stories seriously (even if not literally)."[24]

That Jesus' resurrection actually occurred as an event in history is "highly improbable" for Borg because such an occurrence is not verifiable within the canons of historical criticism. It would be an event whose causality is transcendent (God), and it would not conform to the principle of analogy, being incomparable to any normal event, resuscitation being the proximate possibility.

Nevertheless, Borg will not rule out the possibility of actual resurrection because he is both critical historian and Christian apologist. The final result is that he tries to have it both ways. As a Christian Borg believes that the "risen Christ...does share all of the qualities of God," even if "the historical Jesus did not."[25] Both Spong and Borg assert that Christianity "works" in the lives of people on a day-by-day basis even though the resurrection is religious fiction. They do not seem to have found a way to assure us that it is true and that Christianity "works," not despite the absence of resurrection but because the resurrection is actually true knowledge. What Borg calls the "new vision" and what Spong reconstructs as "more plausible" are not really new at all in essential assumptions. It is little more than a recent version of an old dilemma set in a new context—a modern set of presuppositions still reigning supreme in a postmodern era.

Chapter Four

The Promise of Postmodernity

Pastiche Phenomenology

In the previous chapter we encountered an intentionality quite in keeping with postmodern consciousness, the inclination to bridge what has often been referred to as the split between theory and practice. For Plato the disjunction was between thought and experience, for us it is between theory and practice; and we are still trying to heal the split. It is the attempt of postmodern thinkers to mediate between frames of reference (typically juxtaposed) in order to obtain a greater goal than either might achieve if the domains remain isolated. In a sense this kind of praxis is what the church is always about in its best moments, and it is attempted most often on Sunday morning between ten and noon. David Buttrick, erstwhile professor of homiletics at Vanderbilt Divinity School, describes the task of preaching with theological integrity in the postmodern era as "patchwork phenomenology." While Buttrick may not have any of what follows in mind, in my view patchwork is like a quilt of many colors, shapes, and designs, a plurality of color with a particular design intended only for that quilt. Not quite as distinctly defined are the images of a pastiche. Like patchwork a pastiche may imply an artist as well as artistic design. It too will include many colors, shapes and designs. There will be an incredible amount of diversity in a pastiche, but there may also be purpose in design.

One of the significant components of the pastiche which concerns Christian proclamation is transformation and redemption-centered preaching, and I believe, along with several theologians

67

we have surveyed, that resurrection is crucial to this message. Unlike recent apologists such as Spong and Borg, I hold the conviction that a kerygma void of actual resurrection is not kerygma at all. Furthermore, a church without resurrection preaching has lost continuity with the historic church. With this loss of continuity comes a loss of identity. I am aware that there are other reasons for the identity issue in mainline Christianity besides the theological/historical ones; but I believe the theological ones to be at the heart of the matter.

The way to address these issues is not to do as many conservative evangelicals have done in their teaching and preaching, and act as if the Enlightenment had never happened. In such an ostrichlike posture it is impossible to have much contact with the world around you. This situation is not an easy one. Fundamentalist literalism that insists on certainty and factuality is itself a narrow expression of modernism, a victim of historicism. The irony is that this conservatism is predicated on the historical assumptions of modernism. The typical emphasis on the literal historical factuality of the resurrection as defined by rationalistic historicism is untenable for those who have intellectually traversed the last two hundred years of modern theology and have become aware of its severe limitations, as well as for those who have unconsciously absorbed into the marrow of their being this modern way of thinking. It is on the verge of becoming socially and culturally and, therefore, theologically impotent. In the life of the church, that is, theology and liturgy, it has produced "an ugly ditch" between faith and reason that has in most respects been catastrophic. Most are now well aware that Richard Niebuhr was quite correct when he observed, "The excision of the resurrection tradition from the fabric of the gospel history is followed by the disintegration of the entire historical sequence of the New Testament."[1] This is not a great loss for those who have concluded that there is no historical sequence in the New Testament, but this conclusion is much less secure at the end of the twentieth century than it was at the beginning.

With regard to proclaiming the risen Lord, it seems we have a "damned if you do" and "damned if you don't" dilemma. I have chosen to take the "damned if you do" route, realizing at least some of the difficulties inherent in such an undertaking. It is this decision that brings me to expressions like "pastiche phenomenology" and "re-traditioning the tradition." But it is here that I am skating on the thinnest of ice. First, the contours of a postmodern theological era are only just beginning to take shape in my thinking. This requires that I think, plan, and shape my emerging theological perspective while I am all the time both preacher and theologian.

As a Christian apologist I am quite comfortable, following Borg when he says he has always been thinking about and praising God, maintaining that our theologizing should be done *in the presence of God*—not in some detached state of disinterest. Also, I proceed with the assumption that my theologizing should strive to be consciously grounded christologically in the Christian Scriptures, and these are to be interpreted *sensus literalis,* something quite different than Fundamentalist biblicism or literalism. In christologically centered theologizing, *sensus literalis,* in Hans Frei's words, "applies primarily to the identification of Jesus as the *ascriptive* subject of the descriptions or stories told about and in relation to him." This holds "whether the status of this identification is that of chief character in a narrative plot, historically factual person, or reality under an ontological scheme." This means that " 'literal' is not referentially univocal" but may embrace several possible perspectives. The hermeneutical point of this is that "the subject matter of these stories is not something or someone else, and that the rest of the canon must in some way or ways, looser or tighter, be related to this subject matter or at least not [be] in contradiction to it." In the interpretation of Scripture, "the literal sense has priority over other legitimate readings, be they allegorical, moral, or critical."[2] Or, I might add, midrashic. In the Jesus research sketched above, there was a line of interpretation running through our narrative that represents a consensus of modern scholarship: *the literal ascriptive mode* about *Jesus does not apply to the* reality status *of the ascriptive subject Jesus.* On this point I part company with that consensus. Due to the grip of historicism on interpretation, scholars have been constitutionally incapable of ascribing any level of normative status to the relationship of the stories about Jesus' activities with the actual being of Jesus. Now, if the modern period is really over, if we really are in a postmodern period, then maybe, just maybe, we postmodern people are no longer *incapable* of allowing for the legitimacy of this relationship. Perhaps we are beginning to perceive that

69

there are other criteria for truth and factuality than those prescribed by the canons of historical analysis.

The use of *sensus literalis* indicates that I am not advocating a return to biblicistic literalism, and there is another dimension that is vital to my proposed postmodern perspective, namely, an elementary application of phenomenology. As I do this, I am consciously working from the frame of reference that Frei describes as a type four theology:

> That Christian theology is a nonsystematic combination of normed Christian self-description and method founded on general theory... [and] the practical discipline of [this] Christian self-description governs and limits the applicability of general criteria of meaning in theology.... There can be no ultimate conflict between them, but in finite existence and thought we cannot know [in a final and complete way] how they fit together in principle. As a result, Christian doctrinal statements are understood to have a status similar to that of grammatical rules implicit in discourse, and their relation to the broader or even universal linguistic or conceptual context within which they are generated remains only fragmentarily—perhaps at times negatively—specifiable; yet it is important to keep that relation open and constantly restate doctrinal statements in the light of cultural and conceptual change.[3]

Within this methodological frame of reference, I suggest exercises in what I loosely describe as pastiche phenomenology. In this exercise we do not get the image in a comprehensively clear and final focus, but neither are we lost in disjunction and contradiction.

In order to get adequate images it is incumbent on the preacher/ theologian to go back initially (and primarily) to at least two sources for his/her content—first, the Scriptures, especially the narrative(s) and story(ies) about Jesus, but also the traditions from the Old Testament that the New Testament writers appropriated and personified, such as servant, suffering servant, wisdom, etc. We go back to these using all the viable resources that our linguistic and historical tools have placed at our disposal. We also go back—we must go back—to the tradition(s) that gave rise to the historic faith, that gave rise to our faith, if we really expect to be party to the coming generations of new faith—the explicit goal and purpose of transformational proclamation and redemption.

As we return in the presence of God to these traditions, we apply the first and foundational principle of phenomenology to our enterprise—we consciously set aside our known preconceptions and notions. In this case, as a postmodern people, we mentally set aside the canons of historical verification that by definition render impossible the idea that there is a connection between the literal ascriptive stories about Jesus and the actual being of Jesus. We go to the Scriptures and let the story, the phenomena, speak for itself. We go not to one story or even to several stories, we return to the entirety of the story with an openness to the reality that the writers themselves clearly believed lay behind the accounts. Setting aside any historicist assumptions that might render the accounts unbelievable, we enter the thought world of the early writers. Our intention is to "get inside" their frame of reference. By "indwelling" these accounts we see into the experiences of earlier believers, and our experience joins theirs to give us the beginnings of our pastiche.

You will have noticed that I have varied between singular and plural, story and stories, narrative and narratives, account and accounts. This vacillation is in itself a reflection of historical analysis, but I believe that when we pursue this diligently over a period of time, a pastiche of these phenomena appears. The testimony of the Christian church over two millennia is that when we theologize in the presence of God, whether behind the pulpit or the lectern, the coherence of the phenomena and the ground reality out of which they arise becomes apparent. The story becomes the reality, and in that moment it is the idea that there is any disjunction between the stories *about* Jesus and the *theandric reality of Jesus* that becomes nonsensical and irrational. For those before who kept the traditions alive and to those who wrote them down for us to read, the Christian tradition was impassioned God-Speech. From beginning to end, there is hardly a phrase in Scripture that is cool, detached, and dispassionate, for these writings which are a model of interactive communication, were intended to preserve, yes, but also to persuade the present and future generations to walk in *the way*. This is also the case for doctrinal formulation and gospel proclamation. There is coherence and there is design in the story(ies), and with all the diversity, the soteriological design in the pastiche becomes more readily apparent when the reader or listener allows the phenomena to

71

speak with the intentionality of the proclaimer. Amid the incredible diversity of perspective that characterizes the accounts, the artistry of the soteriological intention is never lost.

But it is not enough simply to repeat the words of the tradition; it must always be re-traditioned. And I do *not* believe that the best way for us to do this is to vault over two thousand years of theological development to the twenty-first century with a barrage of sociological and psychological application. We must first consciously re-tradition our tradition through increased familiarity with the communities of faith to which the soteriological phenomena have given rise. This means that in addition to Scripture, we must engage intentionally and intensely the subsequent traditions. In this historical immersion, also an exercise in pastiche phenomenology, it is more than mere symbolics—simply reading the creeds and formulae. We do our best to enter the thought world of the writers and allow their assumptions and intentionality to speak. We engage first in an anamnesis (re-membering) of symbolic theology, in which we so identify with the source that we learn to think their thoughts and feel their feelings. We allow the reality that gave rise to their faith to become a present reality.

When we have done this with Scripture, and when we have done this with the subsequent traditions, then we can engage in contemporary symbolic theology, re-traditioning the tradition for our generation. We can then engage in God speech that arises out of a convictional identity that parallels the intensity of the Evangelists of the first, second, and subsequent centuries. When we have freshly engaged in these exercises, then our re-traditioning of the tradition, rather than being the dead faith of the living, becomes the living faith of the dead.

Overcoming Objectification

In order for us to even be able to read Scripture and tradition "openly" as has been described above, without trying to force what we read into an objectified account of reality, we must unlearn an entire way of thinking—one in which every part must fit logically and rationally into a clearly defined whole. For purposes of reference, we call this habit "objectification." The last three hundred years, until very recently, have been characterized by this tendency, and it has more or less taken up personal residence in our frames of reference. This old epistemology has taught us that personal and emotional involvement are hindrances to knowing truth; cool detachment is the proper attitude.

Parker Palmer has correctly observed, "Objectivism begins by assuming a sharp distinction between the knower and the objects to be known. These objects exist 'out there,' apart from and independent of the knower. They wait, passive and inert, for us to know them. We, the knowers, are the active agents. We move into the field of objects equipped with tools that allow us to grasp them. Then we attempt to observe and dissect the objects by means of empirical measurement and logical analysis."[4] It is not Parker's intention to engage historicism in its theological manifestation, but he has described for us the reigning frame of reference with regard to the life, death, and resurrection of Jesus. Witness the Jesus Seminar's voting by colored beads to find a consensus on what Jesus did or did not say. The cool detachment reflected in this voting process reduces truth and knowledge to a form of spectator sport.

The agenda for objectivism is to eliminate all elements of subjectivity, all biases and preconceptions, so that our knowledge can become purely empirical. For the sake of objectivity, our inner realities are factored out of the knowledge equation. This is why, even today, the professor is active and the student is passive in many university classrooms. The teacher is qualified to represent the facts because he or she has overcome subjective bias through long years of training. In Palmer's words, "The students have not yet achieved this state of grace; they are still under the influence of emotions, prejudices, and whims."[5] The professor's role is to teach the students the facts; the student's role is to learn the facts: "I tell. You write. You rehearse these facts, at midterm and on the final exam."

Anything that can be counted as true must conform to this paradigm of factuality, capable of isolation and verification by empirical, rational, and logical method. Should you bring something forward that does not conform, this, by definition, cannot possibly be true. We gain mastery (objective knowledge) over whatever is brought to the table by submitting it to our hermeneutic of suspicion and doubt: *It can be judged to be true if... but it cannot be true unless....* In so doing we have limited *a priori* what can and what cannot be true. It is at this juncture that I am suggesting that we exercise an elementary understanding of phenomenology by "bracketing" the Cartesian assumptions. We respectfully entertain our doubts, but we are not required to be negatively suspicious. We are not discarding the inclination to question, but we are suspending judgment.

Peter Berger has suggested that we may move forward epistemologically if we will allow the application of what we know as the sociology of knowledge. The fundamental axiom at work in this sociology is this: you must assume something is true in order to know whether anything at all is true. You may, in fact, assume that several things are true even if they seem contradictory. The goal of this sociology of knowledge is to obtain some level of coherence. In his *Rumor of Angels,* Berger criticized the manner in which objectivist thinking had sought to invalidate the reality of a religious view of the world. He used the sociology of knowledge to "relativize the relativizers." Subsequently, in *The Heretical Imperative,* Berger continued his assault on modernity, spelling out in some detail how the sociology of knowledge allows three avenues of response to modernism: deduction, reduction, and induction. We always have choices. Indeed, says Berger, "One of the elements of modern consciousness that is very hard indeed to 'think away' is . . . the multiplication of options." Put differently, postmodern consciousness requires a movement from prescribed possibilities to multiple options. To decide means to reflect. The postmodern individual must stop and pause where premoderns could act with cool certainty. We live in a world of institutionalized pluralism. In Berger's words, "The typical situation in which the individual finds himself in a traditional society is one where there are highly reliable plausibility structures. Conversely, modern societies are characterized by unstable, incohesive, unreliable plausibility structures. Put differently, in the modern situation certainty is hard to come by."[7]

The intellectual constructs through which we can strive for this elusive certainty are three in number.[8] In the face of postmodern secularity and pluralism, deduction is the *a priori* assertion of traditional religious authority as our guide. In Berger's words, "The deductive option has the cognitive advantage of once more providing religious reflection with objective criteria of validity. The major disadvantage is the difficulty of sustaining the subjective plausibility of such a procedure" in our context (p. 62). This is the option used by those who proudly wave the flag of Fundamentalism.

Our second option is reduction—reinterpreting the tradition in terms of our postmodern assumptions. This can be done in varying degrees, but the end result is typically the same. We saw an example of this in Bishop Spong. Berger explains that "the reductive option . . . is marked by something more radical than the employment of this or that modern intellectual tool," such as historical-critical exegesis. It has most often resulted in "an exchange of authorities: The authority of modern thought or [postmodern] consciousness is substituted for the authority of tradition, the *Deus dixit* ["God says"] of old replaced by an equally insistent *Homo modernus dixit* ["The modern person says"]. In other words, modern consciousness and its alleged categories become the only criteria of validity for religious reflection. These criteria are also given an objective status, insofar as those who take this option tend to have very definite ideas as to what is and what is not 'permissible' " for us to affirm as truth. "Taking this option opens up a cognitive program, by which affirmations derived from the tradition are systematically translated into terms 'permissible' within the framework of modern secularity" (p. 62). We hear and see only what is believable. The trade-off for this comfortable believability is that "the tradition, with all its religious contents, tend to disappear or dissolve in the process" of absorption into our modern (or emerging postmodern) consciousness (p. 62). The attendant result of this option is the dead end of a totally secularized view of reality. This is not viable for the church. We must live with the *plurality* of our world, but we do not have to succumb to a comprehensive *pluralism* that is characterized by a-religious or anti-religious and thoroughly relativized categories.

This brings us to our third epistemological possibility: Induction. This requires that we embrace the plurality of our world and "turn to experience as the ground of all religious affirmations—one's own experience, to whatever extent that is possible, and the experience embodied in a particular range of traditions," such as the church (pp. 62-63). "This range may be of varying breadth—limited minimally to one's own tradition, or expanded maximally to include the fullest available record of human religious history" (p. 63).

75

Groups of individuals or one person may choose to limit the range for reasons related to the interplay of the wide and diverse possibilities, but this does not alter the fundamental assumption: "a deliberately empirical attitude, a weighing and assessing frame of mind—not necessarily cool and dispassionate, but unwilling to impose closure on the quest for religious truth by invoking any [outside] authority," either modern or premodern. "The advantage of this option is its open-mindeness and the freshness that usually comes from a nonauthoritarian approach to questions of truth. The disadvantage, needless to say, is that open-mindeness tends to be linked to open-endedness, and this frustrates [our] . . . religious hunger for certainty" (p. 63).

It is important to note here the caveat that I have included (contra Berger) that a group or individual may decide that certain religious explorations are beyond the pale. While for some this avoidance may be the result of their desire for some level of certainty, for others it may be from motivations of coherence. These two are not the same, but they are clearly related. We cannot hold indefinitely to self-contradictions and retain coherence. While dialectic is unavoidable, inherent contradiction is not viable. *Openness is our attitude; personal and community experience* (past and present) *is our primary venue; and a coherent view of reality is our goal.* Knowledge gained in this way is not cool and dispassionate but highly personal and potentially transformative.

Subscribing to Personal Knowledge

There are a variety of "new" epistemologies across the landscape of postmodern intellectual pursuit that vie for our allegiance. These typically revolve around precepts like story or narrative. Feminist theologians have been the pacesetters in these attempts to overcome the dominant paradigm of objectification. Were more space and time available, we could explore the liberating possibilities inherent in recent feminist creativity. We would also discover, however, that the openness achieved through *many* uses of narrative and story quite often leads to the open-endedness mentioned above: *My story is as valid as your story, so why should one be privileged over the other?* The result is then an expression of pluralistic relativism in which anything goes:

"Different strokes for different folks." This will not suffice. I repeat: The church has no choice but to live with plurality, but we do not have to succumb to a thoroughly relativized pluralism. In a plural world we must make choices, but we do not have to accept recent commonplace assertions that it is no longer possible to make truth claims. It is the case, however, that we cannot credibly make truth claims any longer in the manner in which we once did. The question is, How do we make them?

One of the more sophisticated avenues for claiming truth, avoiding objectification but retaining the personal dimension cherished in story and narrative epistemologies, is to be found in the writings of Michael Polanyi.[9] What Polanyi calls "tacit knowledge" is a "personal knowledge" by which we *know* more than can be objectified. In the Enlightenment epistemologies, as we have seen, it was not allowed that one could know any more than what could be objectified. One might *believe* more than what could be objectified, but only objectified truth was *knowledge*. In Polanyi's thought this self-imposed limitation is transcended, and furthermore, the transcending is accomplished by a "scientist" doing epistemology in a "scientific" manner. What more could one ask!

Polanyi's thought is heuristic, inclined toward the discovery of truth in its rich and varied textures; but this does not mean that objectivity gives way to rampant subjectivity. One of the most important, yet more misunderstood, concepts in Polanyi's thought is his proposal of an alternative to the ideal of objective scientific knowledge, what we are calling objectification. Polanyi deeply believes in objectivity but of a different kind and on a different basis from what is widely understood.[10] I call this an objectivity beyond objectification. He describes for us the essential nature of the scientific outlook that he is trying to overcome: "The declared aim of modern science is to establish a strictly detached, objective knowledge."[11] From the beginning he asserts, "I start by rejecting the ideal of scientific detachment. In the exact sciences, this false ideal is perhaps harmless, for it is in fact disregarded there by most scientists. But we shall see that it exercises a destructive influence in biology, psychology and sociology and falsifies our whole outlook far beyond the domain of science."[12] We recall the manner in which objectification, following Plato's dualism, has held theology captive for almost three hundred years.

Richard Rorty has incisively criticized the reigning epistemology of the Enlightenment derived from Plato, rooted as it is in
his conception of true and necessary knowledge as a kind of mental vision: "There was, we moderns may say with the ingratitude
of hindsight, no particular reason why this ocular metaphor
seized the imagination of the founders of Western thought. But it
did. . . . The notion of 'contemplation,' of knowledge of universal
concepts or truths as θεωρία, makes the Eye of the Mind the
inescapable model for the better sort of knowledge."[13] Rorty's
own view is that the ocular metaphor has led philosophy, and I
would add theology, particularly since Descartes, into a blind
alley, and that we should instead take a pragmatic approach to
knowledge. This move is indispensable to the postmodern era, but
it seems to me that Michael Polanyi has a more comprehensive
epistemological move in view. Gunton observes:

> Polanyi's objections to the old Platonic metaphor are part intellec-
> tual (it distorts) and part moral (it alienates). In particular, by
> viewing the mind as external to the world—contemplating it from
> without, as one might view a landscape from an aircraft—it also
> sees it as impersonal and with pretensions to omniscience. The
> "critical" ideology resulting from the picture makes the mind
> claim too much for some forms of knowledge—those it can, sup-
> posedly, *contemplate* in a totally objective way: truths of reason
> and basic sense experience—and too little for everything else,
> including matters of morality, politics and theology.[14]

Due to limited purpose and scope, we can only touch on one
central value and supposition in Polanyi's epistemology—its
heuristic character. In the old scientific model, discovery and
progress were alleged to come by way of cool detachment. When
Polanyi rejects this, he also demonstrates that its very projection
was, in fact, a delusion. No one really does research by adhering
to a philosophy of science characterized by impersonal detachment. If we did, then discovery would be accidental. A discovery
may come as a surprise accompanied by "Eureka!" but in reality
the researcher entered the routine of established procedures following a promising problem, data, or hunch. The level of subjectivity inherent in this decision is unavoidable. The very nature of
discovery is marked by a personal dimension that is the Achilles'
heel of the objective ideal of "scientific" knowledge at the

assumptive level. For the creative imagination that leads to discovery is no more impersonal than the person making the discovery.

What is the nature of creative imagination that produces scientific discoveries?[15] Polanyi found his clue in Gestalt psychology, but he went a step further. Gestalt teaches that our knowledge is the integration of certain pieces in our perception that we put together to form a whole. Whereas the psychologists chose the mechanistic point as their place to stop, regarding perception to be an internal equilibration of external stimuli, Polanyi went a step further. He added that the seeing of a pattern is the outcome of an *intentional* effort of the person to ascertain order in reality. Put another way, a micro-insight was given a macro-application.

The implications of this insight were far-reaching. It meant that not only was the act of discovery dependent upon the personal powers of thought, it overthrew three centuries of epistemology built upon a structure of knowledge which insisted that personal and subjective levels of participation must be eliminated. The assumption that knowledge could not be personal, that it must be impersonal and objective, is declared invalid. The most basic assumptions of the reigning epistemologies were challenged by an altogether contrary notion: *our knowing is an integration of bodily and intuitive clues that we* indwell *in order to understand.* The cool, dispassionate, and impersonal researcher is not only called into question, it is implied that such a person never existed.

Polanyi went about making his case in the most *personal* way possible. He began to collect cases in which the most traditional scientific rules were flouted. He became, as he describes himself, "a scandal-monger," showing that it was not to the advantage of science to follow its dogma of impersonal, objective knowledge. One of his most striking cases was the story of Einstein's "discovery" of the theory of relativity.[16] According to most physics textbooks, Einstein was led to his theory by the failure of the famous Michelson and Morley experiment of 1887, an experiment which expected to find that the speed of a light signal sent out from a given point would be affected by the motion of the earth. The experiment, however, showed no discrepancy regardless of the direction of the measurement. Working from the objective ideal of knowledge, which holds that science works from observable facts, textbooks said that Einstein set out to find a new conception of space and time to explain the Michelson and Morley experiment.

Actually, Einstein himself indicated in his autobiography that the new theory was primarily a work of his imagination. Incredible as it may sound, he had begun to ponder intuitively the problem of relativity when a schoolboy of only sixteen years. Polanyi wrote to Einstein, and he confirmed in a personal letter to Polanyi that it was indeed an intuitive path that led to the discovery of relativity. When Polanyi published this account in *Personal Knowledge* in 1958, the scientific dogma about Einstein did not go away. In 1963 a prominent philosopher of science said that Polanyi's account was pure invention and that Polanyi's description of Einstein's discovery "was like Schiller's story that his poetic inspiration came to him by smelling rotten apples."[17] Not until 1969, when Gerald Holton confirmed Polanyi's account with evidence based on Einstein's personal papers, did the scientific community concede the priority for Einstein of intuition over scientific objectivity as the place where the discovery began. The most coherent view of reality available to us today began intuitively in the mind of a precocious sixteen-year-old!

The importance of a particular discovery is, of course, surpassed by the nature of making discoveries. Following through the nature of discovery, we are led to a total rethinking of the general idea of knowledge itself. *Discovery is the validating marker, but the nature of the discovery process leads to a truer understanding of knowledge and of ourselves as persons.* Gelwick has asserted that inherent in the structures of Polanyi's heuristic epistemology are three assumptions. Though distilled from Polanyi's thought twenty years ago, they are relevant as ever at this juncture in our society:

> First and foremost is the assumption that we are living in a crisis of civilized culture. It is a crisis that has been developing for at least several centuries, probably one that recurs periodically in every major cultural epoch as each civilization has to decide to renew itself and live or to decay and die. [Polanyi's cultural reference is the "West" in general, but it certainly fits the North American context of the last one hundred years.] It is a crisis of the unifying beliefs and traditions that tie a society together and guide its functional progress. . . .
> A second assumption arises out of the nature of our cultural cri-

sis, namely, the need for a basis of belief upon which we can act. We are in a crisis of belief about belief. Belief itself is discredited by the philosophies and outlooks that guide our present affairs. The impacts of ethical relativism and of scientific materialism have led to doubting any convictions that cannot be readily proved. There is a widespread lack of self-confidence in countering the eroding trends of nihilism. Uncertainty besets the believer in truth and good as ideals for moral conduct because they are lofty, vague, and difficult to define. Against the more obvious evidence of relativism and laboratory tests, the burden of proof appears unbearable.... When the major symbols of meaning today tell us that we are fated to absurdity, we do not attempt to change the situation. At best, we try to live heroically [Sisyphus-like] while the world collapses around us.... We need to know if there is a rational and credible basis upon which we can believe in ideals and goals that are less tangible and incapable of conclusive [scientific, objectified] proof....

The third assumption is that there is a need for grounds for hope that are consonant with a scientific and rational understanding of the world [but not confined to objectification]. Generally, modern science has given us the best understanding of the operation and potentialities of nature.... What is needed is not a revolt against science, technology, or rationality but a new vision of science in which human life and its bond with nature can give us a creative home. Since the world views built upon science are largely responsible for our self-alienation and loss of confidence, it is acutely important that we have a picture in which we can be at one with both a scientific understanding of reality and the highest aspirations and beliefs of humanity.[18]

Polanyi's theory of knowledge and discovery is a fertile field for addressing these issues in our emerging postmodern era. Polanyi fundamentally subverts the distinction between contingent and necessary knowledge, asserting that all human knowledge is contingent and unavoidably rooted in the "knower." He would say to us first that the "knower" *indwells* that reality which waits to be discovered. This is a highly personal understanding that requires the participation of the individual. Detachment is by definition impossible. That which awaits discovery is both "out there" and "inside me" at the same time, or better, "I am in it." Polanyi says that when we are *indwelling* reality we have a *tacit knowledge* of that reality. Imagination and intuition are parts of this, but they are not all there is. In our exploring that which we indwell, we are already in the process of *personal knowing.* As we explore the reality, the tacit knowledge increases. At times the increase is exponential, because what we are learning is not mere fact but rather a knowledge of the structure of reality. In Polanyi's words, I aim for a perspective "in which I may hold firmly to what I believe to be true, even though I know that it might *conceivably* [italics added] be false."[19] In this synergy of discovery and knowing, the whole is always more than the sum of its parts; but we do not have to have all the parts in order to perceive the whole. An actual reality can be affirmed and *known* even if we do not have all the pieces. A pastiche, increasing in clarity, is adequate for our goal, namely, to discover a picture of reality that provides for us a coherent view of life.

Conclusion

I n all of this the questions, and even to some extent the assumptions, inherent in the methodologies of the nineteenth century are still with us as we enter the twenty-first century. To be sure, the sharpness with which these issues cut is still felt keenly in the life of the church, even if they no longer dominate the American Academy of Religion's annual Sears and Roebuck–like catalogue of tidbits for titillation in the month of November. The academic guilds have bequeathed to the church a legacy of cognitive dissonance with regard to gospel, resurrection, and personal redemption, but such arcane items are not listed in the guilds' playbook. This past year in our Church History Group we had learned papers on the topic "Eating Our Way to the Kingdom." The church may not be there yet, but some seem to be willing to take the church into a post-Christian identity—a fallacy largely of our own making. After two hundred years of deconstructing the gospel of resurrection and personal redemption, it is little wonder that a bereaved bishop says to his grieving son, *I do not know, son. I just do not know.* If we do not know at the graves of our grandchildren, do we really *know* every Sunday when we lift the Cup saying, "Christ has died. Christ is risen. Christ will come again"? Is there a way of knowing that can relieve our cognitive dissonance? There is, but in order to get there we must relearn ways of knowing, and then we must re-tradition the church.

The bishop in my opening story is still caught in the reigning epistemology of objectification. He can talk about what the church has taught him to *believe,* but he cannot bring himself to affirm knowledge of a fundamental tenet of the Christian faith. Knowledge must be left for the domain of scientific probabilities. Such was Lessing's "ugly ditch," and such are the muddy waters in which a great many people still swim. Historicism, yet alive at the end of our century, has left us with a divided view of reality. For the Christian who *indwells* Scripture and its Traditions, this version of faith versus reason has left us with no way to hold with intellectual credibility that such things as resurrection, personal redemption, and eternal life are actually descriptive of a reality inviting our participation.

We may *believe* such things, but we do not really *know* them, for Enlightenment historicism has precipitated a revolution in the consciousness of Western intellectual pursuits so profound that we were driven to "doubt." As a matter of fact, the "dare to think" of the early Enlightenment evolved into a negative attitude of suspicion toward anything that smacked of traditional verity. Our story about this, as practiced in the theological disciplines, has revealed that most theological positions are reactions to previous ones. (Indeed, this book is an example.) When one scholar makes the sweeping assertion, "All good historical inquiry is objective and without presupposition," the counterclaim comes, "Every researcher has presuppositions." Or take the thesis of dialectical theologians that "Christian faith cannot be dependent on the 'probabilities' of historical research." This dictum is countered by those who insist, "The Christian faith must take the full risk of the ambiguity of the historical."[1] Ironically, all of these claims and counter-claims are potentially both correct and incorrect. Every researcher has presuppositions, but the good scholar knows how to bracket assumptions that might unduly prejudice quality research. The nature of the case we consider requires us to recognize that the real issue is not whether Christian faith is independent of critical historical inquiry but whether faith includes specific historical assumptions and events that may not be confined to or defined by recently accepted (one-hundred-year-old) canons of historical inquiry. In the light of more recent concepts from sociology and theory of knowledge, objectivity requires that we question these earlier assumptions, both as to their level of adequacy to the issue at hand as well as to their general viability at the end of the twentieth century.

During the modern era (the last two hundred years), history has increasingly been viewed as an account of the "objectively factual past." A little more than fifty years ago R. G. Collingwood called this assumption into serious question when he asserted that "objective factual past" is an abstraction. History is meaningful only when it is studied in its own contextuality and in the present context of the student: "History is for human self-knowledge."[2] The implication is not that history becomes a field of thorough subjectivity, but rather that history is a field of meaning rather than a loose collective of objectified data. Objectivity in research and analysis is mandatory, but objectifying information as fact and data cut loose from their context and meaning is of questionable value. In the case of Jesus, death on the cross avails itself to examination by the canons of historical criticism. It was a rather common experience during the Roman era, and death itself is commonplace. Jesus died—so what? Well, the history of the western hemisphere, even the world, cannot accede to "so what?" The meaningfulness ascribed to the death of Jesus is constituent to history as we know it, not just that he died, but that he died in a specific way; and the meaning of these cannot be detached from the brief life of the crucified Nazarene any more than it can be edited out of western history. It would not be "good history" simply to say: "Jesus lived and Jesus died the death of a thief." That is historically true, but it is not factually adequate.

We recall that the Jesus Seminar scholar Marcus Borg found it impossible to speak and write extensively about Jesus without also speaking about God. Researching as a Christian scholar included this indissoluble connection. Such may also be said with regard to cross and resurrection. How can one speak meaningfully about the actuality and meaning of the cross without including the actuality and meaning of the resurrection? Even scholars like Borg and Spong, committed to historical canons, find this impossible to do. They insist on its meaning, but its actuality simply does not conform to their historical guidelines of analogy and empirical causality. It cannot be objectified as fact. Caught in this same dilemma, Karl Barth proposed an objective event beyond scholarship, a special history of Jesus beyond normal history. It is difficult to imagine how one could get more abstract than this. The dilemma of objectification led Bultmann to define resurrection as a "nature miracle," meaning that it did not happen in the time line of history but that its "reality" so permeated the lives of the disciples that their deep disappointment at the crucifixion was transformed into exultant jubilation at the thought of his resurrection. One cannot help feeling that Bultmann asked us to accept that the disciples believed in a figment of their imagination. The neo-Bultmannianism of James Robinson moved us in the direction of meaning, but meaning is lodged in "how Jesus viewed himself" rather than in the meaning of resurrection itself. Rather than trying to deal with the "problem" of his predecessors, Robinson assumed Bultmann's answer and left the actuality and meaning of resurrection unaddressed.

The church cannot be content to leave the resurrection's actuality and meaning unaddressed, stopping the story with the crucifixion and the symbol of the cross. The fundamental problem with such a move is that the Christian Scriptures are just as concerned, perhaps even more so, with what happened to Jesus after his death as before. The synoptic Gospels comprise only a relatively small amount of the content of the New Testament, and the rest is for the most part either a witness about (not to) the resurrection or a proclamation of the resurrection as the central salvific event.

As long as Christianity takes its scriptures seriously, we will not be able to avoid the unified function and meaning which the cross and resurrection play in Christian identity. If suppositions of some research tend to dis-member this unity, we are required to ask whether other avenues are available. Rather than separating the cross as "allowed fact" from resurrection as disallowed, thereby dissolving the meaningfulness of the double event, perhaps we can move in the same direction as the first generation of believers. The historical product of the indivisible cross-resurrection event, even before the death of the first generation of believers, was a community of believers. Even before the "body of Christ" took on an organized form, it was a living organism of transformed persons sharing their knowledge of and faith in the crucified-resurrected Lord. The *Geschichte* (meaning-filled history) which the early disciples experienced could not be separated from the *Historie* (actual history) which they remembered. Adopting the categories of Collingwood to our purposes, we might express it thus: "The past became a living past, and the past, thereby, became known to the present."[3] Not all the early believers had seen the resurrected Lord—indeed, no one saw him rise—but there is little doubt that the resurrection was accepted and known as actual event. The basis for this acceptance was not "factual data" but "factual experience," the personal and transformative presence in the church of the resurrected Lord, indwelt and known by the believing community.

The history of the Christian church is characterized by remembrance, remembering the living Christ as consistently described, both in apostolic witness and in subsequent record. Any personal history of the present reality of Christ is impossible without remembering this past. All attempts to confine meaning to the present must result in cutting oneself off from the past, and in such an isolation the church would be in grave danger of meaninglessness—for without a referent there is no stability. The Christian church is a significant part of history because the church has insisted that crucifixion-resurrection is an actual part of history. When we remember what the church has consistently remembered about this event, we know what the church has always known. This is a resurrection knowledge that is constitutive both of the meaning and of the very being of the church.

Perhaps bringing into bold relief a "prescription" that is embedded in this essay will bring some relief to the pain in this existential dilemma of our own making in which resurrection knowledge has been difficult for so many:

1. Take seriously that the dualism formalized by Plato and engrained in Western theology since the Enlightenment, an epistemology which insists on true knowledge as mental vision (pure rationality) and subjugates personal and community experience (either present or historic) as second rate, is thoroughly outdated and inadequate to the phenomena of meaningful human existence.

2. Avail ourselves of an elementary application of phenomenology, by bracketing the assumption that things are impossible which do not fit the assumptions of historicism—things like resurrection. After all, if the theory of relativity is true, if all matter is energy, then decomposition and rapid recomposition of life forms is simply a matter of time—no pun intended. Besides, the very idea of God never did fit the principle of analogy: *There is none beside Thee.* If we are going to give up one possibility, resurrection, why not give up both? We Christians got both of these ideas—God and resurrection—from the same places, Scripture and the believing community.

3. Set aside as a permanent value and assumption that true and

intellectually respectable knowledge can only be known by scientific paradigms that are characterized by objectification. This is, in fact, no longer tenable as a reigning epistemological assumption. What will replace objectification as a reigning paradigm is not yet clear, but the notion of detached and disinterested objectivity must be left behind.

4. Be open to the possibility that *knowledge* is available by indwelling a reality that is simultaneously indwelling us—and that this knowledge is as true as any available to us.

5. Affirm the viability of the idea that personal knowledge can begin intuitively and proceed to tacit knowledge through the orderly exploration of the reality that is in the process of being discovered. Objective criteria govern this process, but the learner is not obligated to declare personal detachment from the issues that are at stake.

Historic Christianity has provided to the generations a collection of stories, narrative, and poetry that we know as Scripture. These are not *mere* history. The authors were grounded in what we have defined as personal knowledge and tacit knowing—a reality that provides for the "knower" a certainty that far exceeds the mathematical probabilities of scientific trial and error. It is a view of reality that comes increasingly into clearer focus, characterized by coherence and correspondence. It provides a coherence of meaning as well as a correspondence to the reality out of which it arises. Following biblical injunction we might modify this to *an ever increasing coherence of meaning as well as a growing proximate correspondence to the reality out of which it arises,* for now we see "through a glass darkly . . . but one day we shall know as clearly as we are known." We used to call this a *faith* to live by; it still is, but can we now bring ourselves to *say* what the *communio sanctorum* at its best moments has always known? It is also *true,* and therefore *knowledge* to live by! It is a participative knowledge in God that is redemptive. We can affirm that we *know* this, at the graveside and at the Lord's Table: *Christ has died; Christ is risen; Christ will come again.*

Notes

1. The Eclipse of Gospel Remembrance

1. I have "corrected" *man* to read *humanity* here, intending originally to avoid grating on contemporary sensibilities by changing all the references from cited literature of previous centuries. This proved to be too cumbersome, for writer and reader alike, so for the most part the exclusive language has not been altered.

2. Immanuel Kant, *Die Religion innerhalb der Grenzen der blossen Vernunft*, 2nd ed. (1794), p. 197, quoted by Karl Barth in *Protestant Thought: From Rousseau to Ritschl* (London: SCM Press, 1959) p. 152.

3. Gotthold E. Lessing, *Lessing's Theological Writings: Selections in Translation*, trans. Henry Chadwick (Stanford, Calif.: Stanford University Press, 1957), pp. 17-18.

4. A detailed discussion of these two centuries may be found in the 1962 doctoral dissertation of Daniel P. Fuller written at the University of Basel under the direction of Professors Bo Reicke and Oscar Cullmann, published in the U.S. as *Easter Faith and History* (Grand Rapids: Eerdmans, 1965).

5. Lessing, *Theological Writings*, pp. 51-59.

6. Ibid., p. 53.

7. For a more complete discussion see Colin Gunton, *Yesterday and Today: A Study of Continuities in Christology* (Grand Rapids: Eerdmans, 1983), pp. 139-67.

8. Lessing, *Theological Writings*, p. 55.

9. See especially Kant's *Religion Within the Limits of Reason Alone*, trans. and ed. T. M. Green and H. Hudson (Chicago: Open Court Publishing, 1934).

10. Ibid., p.59.

11. Ibid.

12. Ibid., p. 57.

13. Quoted by Albert Schweitzer, *The Quest of the Historical Jesus*, 2nd ed., trans. W. Montgomery (London: A. & C. Black, 1911), p. 51.

14. Schleiermacher, *The Christian Faith*, ed. H. R. Mackintosh and J. S. Stewart. trans. D. M. Baillie et al. (Edinburgh: T. & T. Clark, 1928), para. 4.3.

15. Ibid., para. 4.4.

16. Schleiermacher, *On Religion: Speeches to Its Cultured Despisers*, trans. John Oman (New York: Harper & Row), 1958. p. 64.

17. Hegel, *The Philosophy of History*, trans. J. Sibree, ed. R. M. Hutchins (Chicago: Encyclopedia Britannica, Inc., 1952), p. 306 col. a.

18. Ibid., pp. 303-9.

19. Ibid., p. 308 col. a.

20. Hegel, *On Christianity: Early Theological Writings*, trans. T. M. Knox (New York: Harper Torchbooks, 1961), p. 292.

21. Strauss, *Life of Jesus*, 2nd ed., trans. George Eliot (New York: Macmillan, 1892), p. 85.

22. Ibid., p. 742.

23. Karl Lachmann, "De ordine narrationum in evangeliis synopticiis," *Theologische Studien und Kritiken* 8 (1835): 570-90.

24. Heinrich Julius Holtzmann, Die *synoptischen Evangelien* (Leipzig: Wilhelm Engelmann, 1863), p. 475.

25. Ibid., p. 459.

26. Holtzmann, *Lehrbuch der neutestamentlichen Theologie,* 2nd ed., 2 vols. (Tübingen: J. C. B. Mohr [Paul Siebeck], 1911), cf. esp. 1:341-42., 379-80., 423, and 431.

27. Albrecht Ritschl, *The Christian Doctrine of Justification and Reconciliation,* 2nd ed., trans. H. R. Mackintosh and A. B. Macaulay (Edinburgh: T. & T. Clark, 1902), p. 469. This English translation is from the 3rd edition (1888) of *Die christliche Lehre von der Rechtfertigung und Versöhnung.*

28. Ibid., pp. 450-51.

29. Ibid., pp. 2-3.

30. Hermann, *The Communion of the Christian with God.* 2nd ed., trans. J. Sandys Stanyon (New York: G. P. Putnam's Sons, 1906), p. 59. This edition was altered and enlarged according to the 4th edition of *Die Verkehr des Christen mit Gott* (Stuttgart, 1903).

31. Ibid., pp. 84-85.

32. Ibid., p. 76.

33. Ibid., pp. 65, 74, 83, 103, 235-36.

34. Johannes Weiss, *Die Predigt Jesu vom Reiche Gottes,* 2nd ed. (Göttingen: Vandenhoeck & Ruprecht, 1900).

35. Wilhelm Wrede, *Das Messiasgeheimnis in den Evangelien,* 3rd ed. (Göttingen: Vandenhoeck & Ruprecht, 1963).

36. Martin Kähler, *Der sogennante historische Jesus und der geschichtliche, biblische Christus* (Theologische Bucherei, 2), ed. E. Wolf (Munich: Chr. Kaiser Verlag, 1956), a reprint of pp. 1-95 of the 2nd ed. of 1896. Trans. and ed. Carl E. Braaten as *The So-Called Historical Jesus and the Historic, Biblical Christ* (Philadelphia: Fortress Press, 1964).

37. Cf. Ernst Troeltsch, *Die Absolutheit des Christentums* (Tübingen: J. C. B. Mohr, 1902), pp. 1-10, and *Gesammelte Schriften* (Tübingen: J. C. B. Mohr, 1913) vol. 2, pp. 729-53. For the English reader a concise and programmatic survey is available in Troeltsch's article "Historiography" in *Encyclopedia of Religion and Ethics,* ed. James Hastings (New York: Charles Scribner's Sons, 1914), vol. 6, pp. 716-23.

38. Kähler, *Der sogennante historische Jesus,* p. 106. My page citations are from the 2nd German edition (1896), edited by Wolf.

39. Albert Schweitzer, *Das Messianitäts- und Leidens-geheimniss: Eine Skizze des Lebens Jesu* (Leipzig, 1901), trans. Walter Lowrie as *The Mystery of the Kingdom of God* (London: A. & C. Black, 1914). The page numbers in the next paragraph are from the English edition.

40. Albert Schweitzer, *Von Reimarus zu Wrede: Eine Geschichte der Leben Jesu Forschung* (Tübingen: 1906), trans. W. Montgomery as *The Quest of the Historical Jesus* (London: A & C. Black, 1910). The page numbers in the next paragraph are from the 2nd edition of the translation, 1911.

2. Giants in the Land

1. Adolf von Harnack, "Rede zur deutsch-amerikanischen Sympathie-kundgebung," in *Aus der Friedens- und Kriegsarbeit* (Giessen: Alfred Topelmann, 1916), p. 288.

2. *Frankfurter Zeitung [The Frankfurt Times],* 4 October 1914, p. 2.

3. Karl Barth, "Evangelical Theology in the 19th Century," *Scottish Journal of Theology Occasional Papers* 8 (1959): 58.

4. Karl Barth, *The Epistle to the Romans* (London: Oxford University Press,

1933), p. 10. Trans. Edwyn C. Hoskyns from *Der Römerbrief,* 6th ed. (Munich: Chr. Kaiser Verlag, 1928). (In the paragraphs that follow the page numbers in the text are from this commentary.)

5. Barth, *The Resurrection of the Dead* (New York: Fleming Revell, 1933), trans. H. J. Stenning.

6. R. Bultmann, "Karl Barth, 'Die Auferstehung der Toten,'" in *Glauben und Verstehen* (Tübingen: J. C. B. Mohr, 1933), vol. 1, p. 54.

7. Cf. especially, *Dogmatics,* I/2, 114-18; III/2, 442-47, 452, 624-33, although it is probably tenuous to continue references to an "early" and a "later" Barth. See note 12 below.

8. See the discussion by Van A. Harvey, *The Historian and the Believer: The Morality of Historical Knowledge and Christian Belief* (New York: Macmillan, 1966), pp. 153-59.

9. We refer the reader especially to the essay by Barth "Rudolf Bultmann—An Attempt to Understand Him" in *Kerygma and Myth: A Theological Debate,* ed. Hans-Werner Bartsch, trans. R. H. Fuller (London: S.P.C.K., 1972), vol. 2, pp. 83-132; and the III/2 section in *Church Dogmatics,* esp. para. 47.

10. Karl Barth, *Church Dogmatics,* ed. G. W. Bromiley and T. F. Torrance (Edinburgh: T. & T. Clark, 1960), III/2, p. 442. (The following quotations, unless otherwise noted, are from this volume of the *Church Dogmatics.* Therefore they will be in parentheses in the text.)

11. Harvey, *The Historian and the Believer,* p. 158.

12. Barth, *Kirchliche Dogmatik,* I/1, 182; *Church Dogmatics* I/1, 175. Recently Bruce L. McCormack, *Karl Barth's Critically Realistic Dialectical Theology* (Oxford: Clarendon Press, 1995), has issued a clarion call for interpreters of Barth to move beyond Hans Urs von Balthasar's "analogy" interpretation of Barth. The perspective offered by McCormack, in harmony with the German scholarship of Gerhard, Sauter, Ingrid Spieckermann, Michael Beintker, Werner Ruschke, and Herbert Anzinger, was suggested a quarter century ago by the late Dutch systematician Hendrikus Berkhof. In seminar he described Barth to us as a "Hermannian of a higher order," by which he meant that Barth was a dialectical theologian of a higher order than his former professor, Wilhelm Hermann. Berkhof later used this descriptive phrase in *Zwei Hundert Jahr Theologie*; English title, *Two Hundred Years of Theology* (Grand Rapids: Eerdmans, 1989), p. 201.

13. McCormack, *Karl Barth's Dialectical Theology,* p. 465.

14. Rudolf Bultmann, *History and Eschatology* (Edinburgh: The University Press, 1957), p. 155. Published in the U.S. as *The Presence of Eternity* (New York: Harper & Row, 1957).

15. Ibid.

16. Barth, "Bultmann—An Attempt," p. 84.

17. Bultmann, in *Kerygma and Myth,* I, pp. 191-211.

18. Ibid., p. 191. Compare also "Das Problem der Hermeneutik," *Zeitschrift für Theologie und Kirche* 47 (1950): 47-69.

19. Cf. "Bultmann Replies to His Critics," p. 191.

20. Cf. Günther Bornkamm, "The Theology of Rudolf Bultmann," in *The Theology of Rudolf Bultmann,* ed. C. W. Kegley (London: SCM Press, 1966), pp. 5-15.

21. Unless otherwise noted the following citations are from Bultmann's essay "New Testament and Mythology" in *Kerygma and Myth,* vol. 1, pp. 1-44. The page numbers will be given in the text in parentheses.

22. Cf. Edwin M. Good, "The Meaning of Demythologization," in *The Theology of Rudolf Bultmann,* pp. 24-25.

23. Ibid., p. 29.

24. Ibid., pp. 32, 34.

25. Cf. "New Testament and Mythology," p. 37; *Theology of the New Testament*, Trans. Kendrick Grobel, vol. 1 (London: SCM Press; New York: Charles Scribner's Sons, 1951), pp. 292-306; vol. 2 (1955), pp. 49-55.

26. *Theology of the New Testament*, vol. 1, p. 295.

27. Cf. "New Testament and Mythology," pp. 38-43.

28. Bultmann, *History and Eschatology*, p. 155.

29. Bultmann, "New Testament and Mythology," p. 44.

30. Bultmann, *History and Eschatology*, pp. 151-52; and "Bultmann Replies to His Critics," p. 209.

3. Jesus in American Scholarship

1. Ernst Käsemann, "Das Problem des historischen Jesus," *Zeitschrift für Theologie and Kirche* 51 (1954): 125-53.

2. Rudolf Bultmann, *Theology of the New Testament*, trans. Kendrick Grobel, vol. 1 (London: SCM Press; New York: Charles Scribner's Sons, 1951), p. 43.

3. Cf. Rudolf Bultmann, "Das Verhältnis der urchristlichen Christusbotschaft am historischen Jesus," in *Exegetica* (Tübingen: J. C. B. Mohr, 1967), pp. 445-70.

4. James M. Robinson, *A New Quest of the Historical Jesus* (London: SCM Press, 1959). Page numbers are in the text.

5. Translated and quoted by Robinson from Hermann Diem, *Der irdische Jesus und der Christus des Glaubens*, vol. 215 of *Sammlung gemeinverständlicher Vorträge und Schriften aus dem Gebiet der Theologie und Religionsgeschichte* (Tübingen: J. C. B. Mohr, 1957), p. 9.

6. This restricted use of *historical* may seem to be an unnecessary narrowing of the term, but this is the very point where the "new questers" distinguish themselves from the older liberal quest. The origin of the original quest as rooted in the Enlightenment's attempt to escape the limitations of dogma and gain "access to the whole reality of the past" has been emphasized by Joachim Jeremias, *Der gegenwärtige Stand der Debatte um das Problem des historischen Jesus* (Stuttgart: Calver Verlag, 1960).

7. Cf. The *Sachkritik* advocated here by Bultmann in *Glauben und Verstehen*, vol. 1 (Tübingen: J. C. B. Mohr, 1933), p. 54; also "Reply to the Theses of J. Schniewind" in *Kerygma and Myth,* ed. Hans-Werner Bartsch, vol. 1 (London: S.P.C.K., 1972), p. 112; and *Theology of the New Testament*, vol. 1, p. 295, in reference to exegesis of 1 Cor. 15. For the purpose of our study we compare also the divergent exegesis of Karl Barth, *The Resurrection of the Dead* (New York: Revell, 1933), pp. 131ff.

8. R. Bultmann, "Primitive Christian Kerygma and the Historical Jesus," in *The Historical Jesus and the Kerygmatic Christ,* ed. Carl E. Braaten and Roy Harrisville (New York: Abingdon Press, 1964), p. 23.

9. The following quotations are from Van Harvey, *The Historian and the Believer* (New York: Macmillan, 1966), pp. 102-4.

10. The English translation by John Bowden, *I Have My Doubts,* with the market-seeking subtitle *How to Become a Christian Without Being a Fundamentalist* (Valley Forge, Pa.: Trinity Press International, 1993).

11. H. M. Kuitert, *Zeker Weten, voor wie geen grond meer onder voeten voelt* (Baarn: Ten Have, 1994).

12. Kuitert, *Jezus: nalatenschap van het Christendom, schets voor een Christologie* (Baarn: Ten Have, 1998).

13. The English translation also by John Bowden, *The Resurrection of Jesus: History, Experience, Theology* (Minneapolis: Fortress Press, 1994).

14. *Christian Century* (17-24 June 1998), p. 606.

15. Cf. J. M. Robinson, "The Study of the Historical Jesus After Nag Hammadi," *Semeia* 44 (1988): 45-55.

16. See the influential study by H. Koester, *Ancient Christian Gospels: Their History and Development* (Philadelphia: Trinity Press International, 1990).

17. See Stevan L. Davies, *The Gospel of Thomas and Christian Wisdom* (New York: Seabury Press, 1983), esp. pp. 1-17; more cautious is David Wenham, *Gospel Perspectives*, vol. 5, *The Jesus Tradition Outside the Gospels* (Sheffield: JSOT Press, 1985), esp. pp. 155-75.

18. John Shelby Spong, *Born of a Woman: A Bishop Rethinks the Birth of Jesus* (San Francisco: Harper, 1992), pp. 13, 181-85.

19. Luke Timothy Johnson, *The Real Jesus: The Misguided Quest for the Historical Jesus and the Truth of the Traditional Gospels* (San Francisco: Harper, 1996), p. 33.

20. The page numbers noted in parentheses in the following paragraphs are from Spong's *Resurrection: Myth or Reality? A Bishop's Search for the Origins of Christianity* (Harper: San Francisco, 1994).

21. S. Aarowitz, "Midrash" in *The Jewish Encyclopedia* (New York: Funk & Wagnalls, 1925).

22. Borg, *The God We Never Knew: Beyond Dogmatic Religion to a More Authentic Contemporary Faith* (San Francisco: Harper, 1997), p. vii.

23. *Jesus in Contemporary Scholarship*, pp. 192-93.

24. *The God We Never Knew*, p. 93, note 39 (p. 106).

25. *Jesus: A New Vision: Spirit, Culture, and the Life of Discipleship* (San Francisco: Harper, 1987), p. 7.

4. The Promise of Postmodernity

1. Richard R. Niebuhr, *Resurrection and Historical Reason* (New York: Charles Scribner's Sons, 1957), p. 14.

2. Hans W. Frei, *Types of Christian Theology* (New Haven: Yale University Press, 1992), p. 5.

3. Ibid., pp. 3-4.

4. Parker J. Palmer, *To Know as We Are Known: Education as a Spiritual Journey* (San Francisco: Harper Collins, 1993), p. 27. Of the works in print, Palmer's work is one of the most sustained pedagogical critiques of Enlightenment objectivism and one of the few which offers a viable alternative.

5. Palmer, p. 35.

6. Peter Berger, *The Heretical Imperative: Contemporary Possibilities of Religious Affirmation* (Garden City, N.Y.: Anchor Press, 1979), p. 11.

7. Ibid., p. 19.

8. See ibid., pp. 60-65. Page numbers given in parentheses in the following paragraphs are from this book.

9. The best introduction to Polanyi is still Richard Gelwick, *The Way of Discovery: An Introduction to the Thought of Michael Polanyi* (New York: Oxford University Press, 1977). Also, Langford and Poteat's introductory essay, "Upon First Sitting Down to Read *Personal Knowledge*..." in *Intellect and Hope*, ed. Thomas A. Langford and William H. Poteat (Durham: Duke University Press, 1968), pp. 3-18, gives an excellent account of the difficulties and unique demands upon the reader of Polanyi's thought.

10. Cf. Michael Polanyi, *Personal Knowledge: Towards a Post-Critical Philosophy* (Chicago: University of Chicago Press, 1958), esp. chap. 1.

11. Michael Polanyi, *The Tacit Dimension* (Garden City, N.Y.: Doubleday, 1966), p. 91.

12. Ibid., p. 20.

13. Richard Rorty, *Philosophy and the Mirror of Nature* (Princeton: University Press, 1980), pp. 38-40.

14. Colin Gunton, *Yesterday and Today: A Study of Continuities in Christology* (Grand Rapids: Eerdmans, 1983), p. 144.

15. Cf. Michael Polanyi, "The Creative Imagination," *Chemical and Engineering News* 44 (April 1966): 85-93.
16. *Personal Knowledge,* pp. 9-11.
17. Cf. Michael Polanyi, "Genius in Science," *Encounter* 38 (January 1972): 46.
18. Gelwick, pp. xii-xv.
19. *Personal Knowledge,* p. 214.

Conclusion

1. This assertion is paradigmatic in the thought of Wolfhart Pannenberg, especially his early writings: *Jesus: God and Man* (Philadelphia: Westminster Press, 1968); and *Revelation as History* (London: Sheed & Ward, 1969).
2. R. G. Collingwood, *The Idea of History* (London: Oxford University Press, 1946), p. 10.
3. See ibid., p. 158.

Selected Bibliography

Aarowitz, S. "Midrash." In *The Jewish Encyclopedia*. New York: Funk & Wagnalls, 1925.

Anzinger, Herbert. *Glaube und kommunikative Praxis: Eine Studie zur "vordilektischen" Theologie Karl Barths*. München: Chr. Kaiser Verlag, 1991.

Barth, Karl. *Church Dogmatics*. 13 vols. Ed. G. W. Bromiley and T. F. Torrance. Edinburgh: T. & T. Clark, 1956–1969.

———. *Church Dogmatics*. 4 vols.; Edinburgh: T. & T. Clark, 1936–1962. Trans. G. T. Thomson and Harold Knight from *Die kirchliche Dogmatik* (I/2-IV/3, Zolliken/Zurich: Evang. Verlag, 1932–1959).

———. *The Epistle to the Romans*. London: Oxford University Press, 1933. Trans. Edwyn C. Hoskyns from *Der Römerbrief*, 6th ed. (Munich: Chr. Kaiser Verlag, 1928).

———. *Protestant Thought: From Rousseau to Ritschl, being the translation of eleven chapters of Die protestantische Theologie im 19. Jahrhundert*. London: SCM Press, 1959.

———. *The Resurrection of the Dead*. New York: Fleming H. Revell, 1933.

———. *The Word of God and the Word of Man*. Trans. Douglas Horton. Boston: Pilgrim Press, 1928.

Bartsch, Hans-Werner, ed. *Kerygma and Myth—A Theological Debate*. 2 vols. in 1. Trans. Reginald H. Fuller. London: S.P.C.K., 1972.

Beintker, Michael. *Die Gottesfrage in der Theologie Wilhelm Herrmanns*. Berlin: Evangelische Verlagsanstalt, 1976.

———. *Die Dialektik in der "dialektischen Theologie" Karl Barths*. München: Chr. Kaiser Verlag, 1987.

Berger, Peter L. *The Heretical Imperative: Contemporary Possibilities of Religious Affirmation*. Garden City, N.Y.: Anchor Press, 1979.

———. *A Rumor of Angels: Modern Society and the Rediscovery of the Supernatural*. Garden City, N.Y. : Doubleday, 1969.

Borg, Marcus J. *The God We Never Knew: Beyond Dogmatic Religion to a More Authentic Contemporary Faith.* San Francisco: Harper, 1997.

———, ed. *Jesus at 2000.* Boulder, Colo.: Westview Press, 1996.

———. *Jesus in Contemporary Scholarship.* Valley Forge, Pa.: Trinity Press International, 1994.

———. *Jesus: A New Vision: Spirit, Culture, and the Life of Discipleship.* San Francisco: Harper & Row, 1987.

———. *Meeting Jesus Again for the First Time: The Historical Jesus and the Heart of Contemporary Faith.* San Francisco: Harper, 1994.

Braaten, Carl E., and Roy A. Harrisville, eds. *The Historical Jesus and the Kerygmatic Christ: Essays on the New Quest of the Historical Jesus.* New York: Abingdon Press, 1964.

Bultmann, Rudolf. *Exegetica: Aufsätze zur Erforschung des Neuen Testaments.* Ed. Erich Dinkler. Tübingen: J. C. B. Mohr, 1967.

———. *Existence and Faith: Shorter Writings of Rudolf Bultmann.* Ed. Schubert M. Ogden. New York: Meridian Books, 1960.

———. *Glauben und Verstehen.* Vol. 1. Tübingen: J. C. B. Mohr, 1933.

———. *History and Eschatology.* Edinburgh: The University Press, 1957. Published in the U.S. as *The Presence of Eternity* (New York: Harper & Row, 1957).

———. *Jesus Christ and Mythology.* London: SCM Press, 1958.

———. *Theology of the New Testament.* 2 vols. Trans. Kendrick Grobel. London: SCM Press; New York: Charles Scribner's Sons, 1951, 1955.

Collingwood, R. G. *The Idea of History.* London: Oxford University Press, 1946.

Davies, Stevan L. *The Gospel of Thomas and Christian Wisdom.* New York: Seabury Press, 1983.

Diem, Hermann. *Der irdische Jesus und der Christus des Glaubens.* Tübingen: J. C. B. Mohr, 1957.

Frei, Hans W. *Types of Christian Theology.* New Haven: Yale University Press, 1992.

Funk, Robert W., Roy W. Hoover, and the Jesus Seminar, eds. *The Five Gospels: The Search for the Authentic Words of Jesus.* New York: Macmillan, 1993.

Gelwick, Richard. *The Way of Discovery: An Introduction to the Thought of Michael Polanyi.* New York: Oxford University Press, 1977.

Gunton, Colin. *Yesterday and Today: A Study of Continuities in Christology.* Grand Rapids: Eerdmans, 1983.

Harvey, Van Austin. *The Historian and the Believer: The Morality of Historical Knowledge and Christian Belief.* New York: Macmillan, 1966.

Hegel, G. W. F. *On Christianity: Early Theological Writings.* New York: Harper Torchbooks, 1961. Trans. T. M. Knox from *Hegel's theologische Jugendschriften,* ed. Herman Noel (Tübingen: J. C. B. Mohr [Paul Siebeck], 1907).

———. *The Philosophy of History.* Trans. J. Sibree. *Great Books of the Western World.* 54 vols. Ed. R. M. Hutchins. Chicago: Encyclopedia Britannica, Inc., 1952.

Hermann, Wilhelm. *The Communion of the Christian with God.* 2nd ed. New York: G. P. Putnam's Sons, 1906. Trans. J. Sandys Stanyon and enlarged and altered in accordance with the 4th edition of *Der Verkehr des Christen mit Gott* (Stuttgart, 1903).

den Heyer, C. J. *Opniew: Wie is Jezus? Balans van 150 jaar onderzoek naar Jesus.* Zoetemeer: Meinema, 1996. Trans. John Bowden as *Jesus Matters: 150 Years of Scholarship* (Valley Forge, Pa.: Trinity Press International, 1997).

Holtzmann, Heinrich Julius. *Lehrbuch der neutestamentlichen Theologie.* 2 vols. 2nd ed. Tübingen: J. C. B. Mohr (Paul Siebeck), 1911.

———. *Die synoptischen Evangelien: Ihr Ursprung und geschichtlicher Charakter.* Leipzig: Wilhelm Engelmann, 1863.

Jeremias, Joachim. *Der gegenwärtige Stand der Debatte um das Problem des historischen Jesus.* Stuttgart: Calver Verlag, 1960.

Johnson, Timothy Luke. *The Real Jesus: The Misguided Quest for the Historical Jesus and the Truth of the Traditional Gospels.* San Francisco: Harper, 1996.

Kähler, Martin. *Der sogenannte historische Jesus und der geschichtliche, biblische Christus.* (Theologische Bücherei, 2.) Ed. E. Wolf. Munich: Chr. Kaiser Verlag, 1956. A reprint of pp. 1-95 of the 2nd edition of 1896. Cf. *The So-Called Historical Jesus and the Historic, Biblical Christ,* trans. and ed. Carl E. Braaten (Philadelphia: Fortress Press, 1964).

Kant, Immanuel. *Religion Within the Limits of Reason Alone.* Trans. and ed. T. M. Greene and H. Hudson. Chicago: Open Court Publishing, 1934. *Die Religion innerhalb der Grenzen der blossen Vernunft,* 2nd ed. (1794).

Kegley, Charles W., ed. *The Theology of Rudolf Bultmann.* London: SCM Press; New York: Harper & Row, 1966.

Knox, John. *The Church and the Reality of Christ.* New York: Harper & Row, 1962.

Koester, Helmut. *Ancient Christian Gospels: Their History and Development.* Philadelphia: Trinity Press International, 1990.

Kuitert, Harry. *I Have My Doubts: How to Become a Christian Without Being a Fundamentalist.* Valley Forge, Pa.: Trinity Press International,

1993. Trans. John Bowden from *Het Algemeen Betwijfeld Christelijk Geloof* (Baarn: Ten Have, 1992).

Lessing, Gotthold E. *Lessing's Theological Writings: Selections in Translation*. Trans. Henry Chadwick. Stanford, Calif.: Stanford University Press, 1957.

Ludemann, Gerd. *The Resurrection of Jesus: History, Experience, Theology*. Minneapolis: Fortress Press, 1994. Trans. John Bowden from *Die Auferstehung Jesu: Historie, Erfahrung, Theologie* (Stuttgart: Radius-Verlag, 1994).

McCormack, Bruce L. *Karl Barth's Critically Realistic Dialectical Theology: Its Genesis and Development, 1909–1936*. Oxford: Clarendon Press, 1995.

Mackintosh, Hugh Ross. *Types of Modern Theology: Schleiermacher to Barth*. London: Nisbet; New York: Charles Scribner's Sons, 1937.

Niebuhr, H. Richard. *The Meaning of Revelation*. New York: Macmillan, 1941.

Niebuhr, Richard R. *Resurrection and Historical Reason: A Study of Theological Method*. New York: Charles Scribner's Sons, 1957.

Palmer, Parker J. *To Know As We Are Known: Education as a Spiritual Journey*. San Francisco: Harper Collins, 1993.

Pannenberg, Wolfhart. *Jesus: God and Man*. Trans. Lewis L. Wilkins and Duane A. Priebe. Philadelphia: Westminister Press, 1968.

———, ed. *Revelation as History*. Trans. D. Granskou and E. Quinn. London: Sheed & Ward, 1969.

Polanyi, Michael. *Personal Knowledge: Towards a Post-Critical Philosophy*. Chicago: University of Chicago Press, 1958.

———. *The Tacit Dimension*. Garden City, N.Y.: Doubleday, 1966.

Ritschl, Albrecht. *The Christian Doctrine of Justification and Reconciliation*. 2nd ed. Trans. H. R. Mackintosh and A. B. Macaulay. Edinburgh: T. & T. Clark, 1902. Translated from the 3rd edition (1888) of *Die christliche Lehre von der Rechtfertigung und Versöhnung*, the third of three volumes on the subject of justification and reconciliation which originally appeared between 1872 and 1874.

Robinson, James M. *A New Quest of the Historical Jesus*. Studies in Biblical Theology 25. London: SCM Press, 1959.

Robinson, James M. and John B. Cobb, eds. *New Frontiers in Theology*. Vol. 3, *Theology as History*. New York: Harper & Row, 1967.

Rorty, Richard. *Philosophy and the Mirror of Nature*. Princeton: University Press, 1980.

Ruscke, Werner. *Entstehung und Ausführung der Diastasentheologie in Karl Barths Zweitem Römerbrief*. Neukirchen-Vluyn: Neukirchener Verlag, 1987.

Sauter, Gerhard. "Die 'dialektische Theologie' und das Problem der Dialektik in der Theologie," in Sauter, *Erwartung und Erfahrung: Predigten, Vorträge und Aufsätze.* München: Christian Kaiser Verlag, 1972, pp. 108-46.

Schleiermacher, Friedrich. *The Christian Faith.* Ed. H. R. Mackintosh and J. S. Stewart. Edinburgh: T. & T. Clark, 1928. Trans. D. M. Baillie et al. from the 2nd edition of *Der christliche Glaube nach den Grundsäzen der evangelischen Kirche* (Berlin: G. Reimer, 1830).

————. *On Religion: Speeches to Its Cultured Despisers.* New York: Harper & Row, 1958. Trans. John Oman from the 3rd edition of *Über die Religion: Reden an die Gebildeten unter ihren Verachtern Schriften,* 4 vols. (Tübingen: J. C. B. Mohr [Paul Siebeck], 1912–1925). 1st ed., 1799.

Schweitzer, Albert. *Das Messianitäts- und Leidens-geheimniss: Eine Skizze des Lebens Jesu.* Leipzig: 1901. Trans. Walter Lowrie as *The Mystery of the Kingdom of God* (London: A. & C. Black, 1914).

————. *The Quest of the Historical Jesus.* 2nd ed. London: A. & C. Black, 1931. 1st ed., 1910. Trans. W. Montgomery from *Von Reimarus zu Wrede: Eine Geschichte der Leben Jesu Forschung.* (Tübingen: 1906).

Spieckermann, Ingrid. *Gotteserkenntnis: Ein Beitrag zur Grundfrage der neuen Theologie Karl Barths.* München: Chr. Kaiser Verlag, 1985.

Spong, John Shelby. *Born of a Woman: A Bishop Rethinks the Birth of Jesus.* San Francisco: Harper, 1992.

————. *Liberating the Gospels: Reading the Bible with Jewish Eyes.* San Francisco: Harper, 1996.

————. *Resurrection: Myth or Reality? A Bishop's Search for the Origins of Christianity.* San Francisco: Harper, 1994.

————. *Why Christianity Must Change or Die: A Bishop Speaks to Believers in Exile.* San Francisco: Harper, 1998.

Strauss, David F. *The Life of Jesus.* 2nd ed. New York: Macmillan, 1892. Trans. George Eliot from the 4th edition (1840) of *Das Leben Jesu.*

Troeltsch, Ernst. *Die Absolutheit des Christentums.* Tübingen: J. C. B. Mohr, 1902.

————. "Historiography." *Encyclopedia of Religion and Ethics.* Vol. 6. Ed. James Hasting. New York: Charles Scribner's Sons, 1914.

————. "Über die historische und dogmatische Methode in der Theologie." In *Zur religiösen Lage: Religionsphilosophie und Ethik,* pp. 729-53. Vol. 2 of *Gesammelte Schriften.* Tübingen: J. C. B. Mohr, 1913.

Weiss, Johannes. *Die Predigt Jesu vom Reiche Gottes.* 2nd ed. Göttingen: Vandenhoeck & Ruprecht, 1900.

Wenham, David. *Gospel Perspectives*. Vol. 5, *The Jesus Tradition Outside the Gospels*. Sheffield: JSOT Press, 1985.

Wrede, Wilhelm. *Das Messiasgeheimnis in den Evangelien*. 3rd ed. Göttingen: Vandenhoeck & Ruprecht, 1963.

Newspapers and Periodicals

Beintker, Michael. "Krisis und Gnade: Zur theologischen Deutung der Dialektik beim frühen Karl Barth." *Evangelische Theologie* 46 (1986): 442-56.

Bultmann, Rudolf. "The New Approach to the Synoptic Problem." *The Journal of Religion* 6 (1962): 337-62.

―――. "Das Problem der Hermeneutik." *Zeitschrift für Theologie und Kirche* 47 (1950): 47-60.

The Christian Century. 17-24 June 1998, p. 606.

Frankfurter Zeitung [The Frankfurt Times]. 4 October 1914, p. 2.

Käsemann, Ernst. "Das Problem des historischen Jesus." *Zeitschrift für Theologie und Kirche* 51 (1954):125-53.

Lachmann, Karl. "De ordine narrationum in evangeliis synopticiis." *Theologische Studien und Kritiken* 8 (1835): 570-90.

Polanyi, Michael. "The Creative Imagination." *Chemical and Engineering News* 44 (April 1966): 85-93.

―――. "Genius in Science." *Encounter* 38 (January 1972): 46.

Robinson, James M. "The Study of the Historical Jesus after Nag Hammadi." *Semeia* 44 (1988): 45-55.

Sauter, Gerhard. "Weichenstellungen im Denken Karl Barths." *Evangelische Theologie* 46 (1986): 476-88.

Index of Names

Index of Subjects